MARK
THAT WORKS
for small business budgets

[Beyond
Social Media]

If you are:

✓ Annoyed every time the gurus insist "social media marketing, content calendars, and consistency" are the key to marketing success on a budget...

✓ Wondering why other small businesses seem to have so much success on social media, but you're just not getting the same results...

✓ Frustrated because you have a better product or service and better customer service, but fewer customers...

this book is for you.

This book is dedicated to all the industry disrupters who refuse to give up. Your marketing deserves to make as big an impact as you do!

Marketing That Works for Small Business Budgets [Beyond Social Media]
ISBN: 978-0-9962288-4-8

TABLE OF CONTENTS

"Stephanie is a master marketer. She's proved time and time again how to innovate and out-think, not out-spend. In *Marketing That Works for Small Business Budgets*, Stephanie leads you through tried-and-true methods of how to think differently and develop marketing strategies that work for YOU and YOUR business. Written in "choose your own adventure" style, this book lays out the blueprint for any small business looking to stand out and change the game in their industry."

Jesse Cole, owner of The Savannah Bananas

"Stephanie markets like few do and gets the results few achieve. Follow her sage advice for your own marketing success."

Mike Michalowicz, author of Get Different and Profit First

How to Navigate This Book
(Especially if you've got ADHD [or think you do]...Read this first!)

Hello there fellow journey-er!

The author here, Stephanie.

If you know anything about me, you know that I'm incredibly passionate about helping small business owners, particularly those like me whose ADHD plays a daily role in their lives. Over the past couple of years, I've discovered that I'm not alone in my weirdness and a lot of the ways I process, internalize and implement information are actually tied to the ADHD I've dealt with my entire life.

That said, I also realize that *you* might internalize information similarly to me. So I'm putting this book together in a way that would help me absorb the information better, and hoping it will do the same for you. A few notes about reading this book:

Craft Your Course - This book is written similarly to the "Choose Your Own Adventure" books that were so popular in the 80s and 90s. At the end of most sections, you'll have the choice of whether to continue reading the book in order, or skip ahead to the section that scratches your brain itch or business needs most![1]

Skimming - I like to skim information to get an idea for what I'm about to learn so I can organize that content in my head. Skim away. Check out headers and bolded text to get a feel for what's to come.

---

[1] Kudos and thanks to Treion Muller for his groundbreaking work with bringing this concept to the personal growth book world with his book *Rise of the Mutant Learner*.

Action items - I'm including specific action items where they are applicable. These are indicated by my signature paint poof under them.

Takeaways - I've marked key takeaway paragraphs in a font concept called **Half-Bo**ld that has some preliminary research behind how well it helps neurodivergent readers absorb and retain information. I've also taken especially valuable quick lines and set them aside in full bold. Pay special attention to these. They are worth re-reading and exploring the nuance of what they mean. These often can be applied far beyond just the application I will discuss in regard to marketing. Consider these a "meditate on it" call to action.

Go Online! I've been obsessed with how to ensure small business owners can take action on what they learned *without* requiring them to purchase tens of thousands of dollars' worth of coaching for nearly a decade now. To that end, I've created a website at MarketingBeyondSocialMedia.com to help support *your* implementation. I've put as many support resources up here as I can and will keep this site updated as I learn more ways to support your entrepreneurial growth!

Let's go!

How Is This Book Different?

The short answer is: This book was written (yes, every word, ghost writers are not my thing) *by* a small business owner working on a very limited marketing budget, *for* small business owners working on very limited marketing budgets. This was written to bring you all the knowledge and practical application that allowed me to double my small events business in size *during* a global pandemic. Grow Disrupt designs and produces "Grow Your Business" style conferences and retreats for ADHD entrepreneurs. It is an industry that was hit particularly hard during the pandemic. There's a lot that went into our ability to stay open and keep hosting in-person events (safely) when most of our world was shut down. But I cannot give enough credit to the guerilla style marketing that kept our events profitable and even helped us achieve sell-out status during a time when many people were beyond freaked out about leaving their homes, much less going to a live event.

This was written knowing that we have to get beyond thinking that social media marketing is the end-all-be-all when it comes to marketing on a budget. Don't get me wrong, I fully agree that there is value in social media for small businesses. It was, and continues to be, a game changer in our marketing world. Social media gives small business owners a platform to speak from that was not accessible twenty years ago. But all too often, that is all small business owners are told to do when it comes to budget marketing. That's a problem because at the end of the day, social media is an amplifier. As such, it rarely works well in isolation. We have to embrace marketing tactics that go beyond whatever social platform is currently most popular.

To be clear, this book is not going to get into the fancy-schmancy analytics and tactics that end up being black holes of overwhelm for most small business owners. I can't tell you how many books I've read that have started with a great idea, but then they start getting into layers and layers of analytics. Suddenly I'm hearing about all kinds of software I need to subscribe to or research in order to find a cheaper alternative, and ultimately nothing ends up getting done. This book was built for the small business owner who is:

1. Trying to get their marketing engine firing while wearing eighteen different hats, AND with an extremely limited budget for marketing and/or
2. Tired AF of navigating a world filled to the brim with people who swear that, for $4,997, $9,997 or $14,997 they can teach you all the tricks of marketing and make you millions.

If that's you, welcome. You're my people!

If you want the long answer, you'll have to keep reading...

How is this marketing book different?
(The Long[er] Answer)

If you're already sold on how excited you are to read this, you can skip this short chapter and get into the good stuff on the next page of Craft Your Course instructions at the end of this section. If you're just picking this up, curious about why to purchase it or how this book is different from the literally thousands of other marketing books out there, keep reading!

I started this book for the same reason I think most authors have: because a hundred people told me that I should write a book on all the stuff I was speaking on (namely, the marketing stuff). But when I first sat down to start fleshing this out, I had a serious moment of imposter syndrome. I do most of my writing up in my office, and off to my left is a decent sized bookshelf of all my favorite books. There's an entire shelf dedicated to my favorite marketing books. Authors like Seth Godin, Dr. Cialdini, Mike Michalowicz, Jesse Cole and Donald Miller have changed my life. Literally. Seth's book *Purple Cow* was the first book I read about marketing and it captivated me enough to make a career out of it! Jesse was the reason I embraced the violin and my ADHD and made it part of my brand which, as you'll see later, caused a cascading effect of growth. Mike's *Get Different book* is what sparked me to really start thinking, well, different when it comes to marketing. Truthfully, Mike's concepts are what prompted me to try the crazy ideas that still leave people shaking their heads at me sometimes[2]. I still revisit many of those books with regularity. (Side note, if you're looking for reading recommendations once you finish this book, I think every small business

_____

2 Like writing and publishing a book that uses Half-Bold fonts and a Craft-Your-Course concept

owner should read *Find Your Yellow Tux* by Jesse and *Get Different* by Mike. They are both perfect extensions of this book because they are both big parts of the impetus for this book!).

So, yes. The first question I asked myself is, "Why on earth am I writing this book? And what do I have to add to the conversation?"

The answer started with recognizing that I've been teaching and refining what works in small business marketing for more than a decade. I've listened and learned from those titans, then applied it in at least a few other businesses, and my own. As a small business owner myself, I am constantly testing what's working and what isn't. I actively dedicate time to keeping up with things as they evolve so I can keep an eye on what's working *today*. Before that, I spent an insane number of hours analyzing and trying to synthesize hundreds of marketing books, classes, and campaign results down into the fewest common denominators. Why? Because I'm a big believer in Einstein's quote that if you can't explain something to a five-year-old, you don't know it well enough. I always thought that if I could figure out the fewest possible components necessary to create marketing that works, it would be reproducible across campaigns, industries, and even countries. I landed on The 3 Ms of Marketing long ago, and over the years I've seen again and again where they are the difference between successful and failed campaigns.

During my moment of, "Am I actually going to do this?", I also realized that, while those books are incredible, with everything else going on daily inside a small business, sometimes it's hard enough to get through one book. Being told to read a small library of books to be successful in marketing is simply unrealistic and daunting. I wanted a book that would highlight the **most important overall lessons** that make marketing work better. Beyond that, I wanted one book that also talks about **how to execute tactics as a whole** and **bring them together into a cohesive strategy**. Importantly, I also wanted a marketing book that makes practical application easy. I'm talking about the step-by-tiny-step instructions needed that are simple enough for even my ADHD, wearing-too-many-hats brain to follow along.

Which brings me to my second reason for writing this book. Since I graduated and entered the workforce, I've been behind the scenes with literally thousands of small businesses and been directly involved with marketing strategy and/or execution for countless campaigns. I've been testing and refining the 3Ms since 2012 when I discovered them. I've had time to look at where small businesses really struggle (including my own!) and had to get creative to solve those problems. In the past few years, my team and I have spearheaded some really cool and impactful marketing campaigns for small business owners, sometimes on budgets as small as a few hundred dollars!

I want other small business owners to know what has worked across those campaigns, both for other brands and our own. I want to share what made Teodoro the Tomato such a huge winner for Capri Housing and how he sprang out of necessity. I want to peel back the curtain on what we did to keep The Grow Retreat as one of the few ongoing and profitable live educational events throughout a global pandemic (and added a second event!). I want to share what's worked in a real-world, to-the-chase way that makes sense for small business owners. But I also want to share what didn't work across the campaigns that I've been privy to so others can avoid making those same missteps.

And I want to bring it all together in one part-book-part-workbook that other small business owners can reference again and again to create their own marketing that works for small business budgets – beyond social media.

If you want the background behind how I landed on these methodologies so you can better understand them for yourself and understand how I know that they work, enjoy a good story or two, or are just still quieting the skeptic on your shoulder, keep reading.

1.

If you want to skip ahead to learn one of the most fundamental truths about marketing I can possibly share with you, skip to **Page 21**

2.

If you want to dig straight into the juicy key to marketing that actually does work on a small budget, skip to **Page 28**

3.

If you want to get straight to the meat and potatoes of how to put together a cohesive marketing plan, on a budget, and come back to the rest later, skip to **Page 53**

"Where did your obsession with small business marketing begin?"

Great question and I think the answer lays the perfect foundation for how my marketing methodologies were tested, and ultimately work best. So, let's start there! And yes, it did start on a snowy street that looked like it was plucked out of a Hallmark movie in central Ohio.

My university experience happened in a small town just north of Columbus, Ohio called Westerville. In the late 2000s and early 2010s, Main Street in Westerville perfectly encapsulated the quintessential small-town charm. Red brick buildings with striped cloth awnings overhung the sidewalks and the windows were decorated with hand-painted art to draw the eye, and hopefully the buyer, into the store. In the winter, when it snowed and the classic black lantern light posts were strung with garlands, I walked up and down the street carrying on vivid conversations in my head as the heroine of my own private Hallmark movie. By my third year, I was noticing that more and more of the locally-owned businesses along the street were being replaced with corporate versions. I remember one cold day in particular that I had to make a trip to CVS to pick up some medication. On my way back to campus, I decided to drop in and check out a local stationary store that had caught my eye a few times. The stationary store had beautiful, locally-made cards alongside some of the more classically accepted "Feel better sooooon!" and "Wishing you the Berry Happiest of Birthdays" cards. The store itself was more thoughtfully laid out and stuffed to the brim with all the extras you'd need when preparing a gift or communicating with someone you care about. Heavyweight envelopes, ribbons, feathers, fountain pens, cards, stamps, and more. It was beautiful.

The CVS had someone on every aisle.

I was the only person in the stationary store.

It was the first time I consciously remember thinking that "if only small businesses could market like the big guys, they'd do just fine!" In my naivety about the world of small business, I figured that a few billboards and TV ads would solve all of a small business's problems.

That moment started an absolute obsession with helping small business owners' market themselves better so they could get the attention they deserve for two primary reasons. Firstly because my parents were and are small business owners. So I had the chance to see the back-end of running a small business first-hand. Secondly because, even as a college student, I recognized that the locally-owned businesses were precious. Scrappy small businesses are the heart of great customer service and the spark of most innovation in the world. Small businesses regularly provide better products and better service than the big brands. Yet the big brands continue to attract the lions share of customers. Why? Because they are known! They may not provide the best product or experience, but at least we know what we'll get when we go to them. And **the human brain has evol**ved **to crave predict**ability! **Afterall, what we've kn**own **in the past hasn't killed us** yet, **so it's clearly safe! At least, th**at's the **assumption our brain makes**. That new business? It's new…it may not be great. So we automatically avoid it to fill a subconscious need for stability in our weird, crazy, wonderful brains.

While that may sound absolutely insane and you may be ready to argue with me about how much you love trying new things, our brains are processing billions of bits of data every single day. Think about how many marketing messages have hit you just today. Let's say it's just barely 7:30am and you're settling in to read a few pages of your cool new marketing book before starting the workday. You probably took a shower and grabbed your branded bottle of shampoo or body wash at some point. Same for the toothpaste. And I'll bet that there was some branding on the coffee package that you used for your morning joe. You may have used a Keurig and your brain noticed the branded logo there. (Or a CoffeeMate, or Cosori kettle and pour-over as is my personal preference!). What did you have for breakfast? Were there branded logos on the products you grabbed? Some Quaker oatmeal? A Jimmy Dean breakfast sandwich? How about the Chiquita sticker on your banana? Did your trashcan have a logo on it that you don't even notice anymore as you threw away your banana peel? Great! Now you've settled down to watch the news and eat breakfast, and your brain is processing a hundred logos and brands in that half hour. The clothes the anchors are wearing, the scrolling text banner, the four billboards shown on the fly-over of the backed-up traffic on the freeway.

It's a lot! And you probably didn't actively remember much of it until I started giving you specific focus-points. The point is that we're inundated with marketing messages daily. And that's not even getting into the millions of messages about how our clothes or that chair feels against the body. Messages that the brain is automatically receiving and filing. Our conscious mind is only able to handle a small fraction of the stimuli we receive. We function most of our life on auto-pilot and base a lot of assumptions on past experiences, with the brain favoring experiences that haven't proven catastrophic yet. I.g.: "That McDonald's hamburger hasn't killed us, and we know what we'll get. What if that hamburger from Joe's Shack up the road ends up being terrible? Or worse, gives me food poisoning? Nah!" My brain settles for safety *automatically* every time. Unless I make a conscious decision otherwise. But that requires me to be consciously aware of the other option. And that requires marketing.

For years I raged against the lack of accessibility to great marketing solutions for small business owners. At one point in time, I harbored a secret wish to become so rich and powerful that I could give away billboard and TV time to small businesses. In lieu of that, I wanted to pass a law that required that any small business who generated less than X in annual revenue be given a discount on those billboards. I won't say that those dreams have entirely faded, but I've learned the problem is incredibly nuanced. And billboards and TV ads don't necessarily solve all the problems in business. I should know, we've tried them.

Why's That? Most small business owners don't know how to design a billboard that will actually convert. Additionally, billboards take a long time to start generating results. Thirdly, no matter how good the marketing, if the sales skills aren't there to back it up, it won't do any good. Marketing also won't make up for a small business owner who can't or won't manage financials and protect margins. Even great marketing will fail when fulfillment can't keep up. And lastly, marketing doesn't make up for the mindsets and training needed for a small business owner to succeed.

In other words: marketing is only as strong as the business it represents.

That said, great marketing does make up for a lot! But it rarely does so overnight. In fact, most of the "overnight success stories" we're familiar with, came at the tail end of a lot of work, brand building, and trial and error.

The challenge is that marketing has gotten more and more complex over the years. Putting your product in a glass jar and taking over the entire marketplace as a result (Looking at you Heinz!) just isn't realistic anymore. We have to be smart about how we're tackling marketing for our small businesses.

Fortunately, while marketing as a whole has grown more and more complex, we're at a turning point where a lot of our tools are getting simpler and simpler to use. The advent of AI and programs like Canva allow us to, without paying a penny, take a solid brand and create some decently professional looking graphic design. Invest in a great logo and a few assets to supplement it (Like my signature 'impact' powder poofs that we put on *everything*).

Understand your message, follow the instructions in this book, and lean into the "guerilla" style that has served so many of us so well! It takes some time and some energy but, as long as you're smart about it, you can make some serious magic happen and make your marketing work like the billion-dollar businesses, on a small business budget!

I'm not going to tell you that massive results are a moment away. Or that you will spend *no* money. Ok, maybe you can get away with spending no money on *ads*. If you're working on a limited budget, I'd rather see you put that money towards content creation, graphic design, and video creation than social media ads anyhow. For most small businesses, straight ad dollars rarely generate sales. The content and conversion funnels just aren't tested and refined enough and the money is usually wasted. **Especially in the early stages**. Instead, we need to focus on creative approaches, testing and refining, and tackling marketing from an educated place in regard to the core components of marketing success. When we do, generating massive marketing results as a small business owner *is* entirely possible, and yes, on a shoestring budget. I've spent more than a decade of trial and error figuring out how, and I'm grateful for the opportunity to help your marketing make more of an impact. I may not be in a position yet to have a billion-dollar fund supplementing the marketing costs of small businesses, but I can do this. And I believe that helping your marketing level up will help position you to thrive both personally and professionally.

As I stated before, I'm a firm believer that small business is the backbone of the world. It's the small business owner who continues providing access to a higher quality of service and products. It's this that keeps big business from being able to get away with cheap products and terrible service built on the backs of slave labor in third world countries (I know, a little dramatic, but also more true than we'd like to accept sometimes). It's small businesses that continue to uphold a higher standard of service and customer care. It's the small, scrappy businesses and entrepreneurs that come up with some of the most incredible, game-changing business ideas on the planet. They spark innovation. They power performance.

Small businesses deserve substantially more attention than they get in the marketplace!

This book exists to help them get it.

Your First Big Takeaway: Time Is NOT Your Greatest Asset

Rather than marking this entire chapter in half-bold I'll just clarify up front: The impact of this takeaway goes way beyond marketing, but since this is a marketing book, we'll be talking mostly about marketing for now. Onto the good stuff!

Even back when I was working my corporate job still, long before starting my first small business and this idea started to become more mainstream, I had a huge revelation: Time is not our greatest asset. I'd heard motivational speakers all talk about how money isn't our greatest asset. But early in 2013, I realized that time was not either. And this is one of the most dangerous concepts that we overlook when it comes to marketing our small businesses. Let's first clear up how I landed on this premise, just in case this is the first time you've encountered this, then we can talk about how it impacts marketing.

Have you ever had an evening where you got home from work and you were just too exhausted to do anything? So instead of doing that workout you planned or making dinner, you ordered pizza and sat on the couch, watching TV or mindlessly flicking through your phone until bedtime? In short, you had time, but no energy to do anything with that time. I understand that we can't get more time, but **without energy, time isn't worth anything**.

Energy is a resource and an asset and as the resource that is in shortest supply, it must be managed well. We have to invest energy into things that give us more energy. This is why it's so important to ensure that we are wasting as little energy chasing dead end ideas as possible. If we get caught in that loop, not only do we then not have energy to pursue our goals, but we also have invested energy in a way that did not bring a return. At this point, we now need more time to recover and refresh. This is not to insinuate that we are able to only do things that generate energy and build a perpetual energy wheel. No matter how carefully we manage our energy, we still need to sleep. But we can do things that lend themselves to being more energized in our next task. We can do things that we love so when we wake up and get to the office, we're enthused to get back to work. We can do things on the weekend that we look forward to so the weekend energizes us for the week. And do things we love during the week so we don't need the whole weekend just to recover from work.

I think most of us realize this instinctively. This is why when marketing is an energy suck not an energy generator, we actively avoid it, because it sucks up the energy that is generated elsewhere. Which means that all the things we love doing in our businesses are countermanded by the black hole of marketing. As a result, we almost universally start avoiding the marketing that is so critical to growth. The dangerous part is that this usually occurs on a subconscious level. Time is blocked out to work on marketing, but "That Thing" pops up. At the end of the day, we don't even remember what "That Thing" was. But it was definitely more important and meant we didn't have time to work on marketing. The problem here? "Build it and they will come" hasn't worked since the 1950s. We need marketing to survive in business. Your potential customers need to know who you are and *remember* you if you want them to buy from you.

Somewhat surprisingly, worse than not doing *any* marketing is when a small business owner forces themselves to push out marketing regardless. Now the marketing that gets pushed out lacks the creative juice that attracts buyers. This leads to the owner feeling like they have to push themselves into doing more marketing, which is just sucking more energy and still not producing clients. Eventually they have no energy left to work on other things in the business. Sooner or later the wheel stops turning entirely.

This is why it matters to me to share both what's worked *and* what hasn't. Because if I can save a small business owner from spinning their wheels and getting frustrated over marketing that isn't working, we can focus our energy on creating marketing that works instead.

This is a theme we'll revisit a few times throughout this book. But for now, suffice to **recognize that time is not your greatest asset. Energy is and it must be protected.**

The First Lesson in Marketing: Market Like a Virtuoso

Don't skip this one. I almost guarantee that this is *not* the concept you think I'm about to break down…

My older sibling and I took piano lessons back when we lived in Alaska. Ari fell in love. I hated it. While Ari sat with our instructor for their lesson, I would wander the store, putzing around on the keyboards and pianos for sale or in the back room watching the store's treasure trove of Disney movies. Eventually I found one keyboard that had the feature I desperately wanted. If I set the keyboard up correctly, I could hit any keys (in any order) and the keyboard would play Für Elise and other classic piano pieces perfectly. I sat at that keyboard a lot, throwing my little body around like I was some great pianist and losing myself in the beauty of the music. Then it would be time for my lesson and I struggled to play Three Blind Mice, much less wrap my head around the music theory homework I managed to lose and failed to complete week after week.

My lessons didn't last more than one or two beginner books before I found an excuse sufficient enough that Mom let me quit. Over the next few years, and across a move back to Texas for Dad's work, my sibling continued their learning. I tweeted my way through (in my mind at least) beautiful renditions of Native American and Andes inspired warbling on my soprano recorder. I loved these because there was no sheet music so every note was the right note. Bless my Mom for not killing me as a kid. When more of my six siblings began to show musical inclinations, I found myself drawn back in. I tried the guitar for one afternoon and quickly decided that it wasn't for me. I returned to the piano only to toss my old books down again quickly. Then at church one evening one of the church members came onstage during prayer to play the violin and I was *captivated*. At the end of the service I hurried over to her and told her how much I loved her playing and lo and behold, she offered to teach me! I was in heaven.

I ordered a cheap violin set online and she helped me set it up at our first lesson where she taught me the fingering and the bow hold. The next week she got orders from the military that it was time to move. It was the first and last violin lesson I got for a very long time, but it was not the last time I picked up the instrument. I printed copious amounts of free sheet music online, refreshed my memory in regards to reading the treble clef, and set myself to playing. I remember one day running out to see my Mom in the kitchen after setting my mind to learn my all-time favorite classical piece (at the time): Pachelbel's Canon in D. I had printed the sheet music only a short while prior and after a few takes through the music, was fairly certain I'd mastered the song. I remember standing in that yellow daisy wall-papered kitchen and bragging about how the violin was supposed to be so hard to learn, but here I was making massive progress, without even having an instructor! To her credit, Mom only smiled and encouraged me to keep practicing.

I, mercifully for my family, upgraded to a (silent) electric violin after a few months. I spent the next few years printing off simple songs for myself and playing on the church worship team. Then I graduated and found myself caught up in life-after-college. Between work and figuring out how to be an adult in a new city then starting my first business, the violin ended up literally buried in the back of my bedroom until one evening early in March 2019.

I remember that night well. I was exhausted. I was drained. I was sitting on my big cream-colored swirly-chair, and desperately wishing it wasn't so late so I could go paint. It had been a long day. I was working on some kind of major project that was due in short order and by the time I finished work, got dinner and ate, it was almost 9pm. I had to be up in a matter of hours to travel for a speaking engagement the next morning and I was craving some creative outlet. However, I knew that by the time I got into the flow of painting (my preferred creative outlet at the time) it would be nearly 10pm and I wouldn't want to stop. I needed something else. That was the moment I realized I didn't have any real hobbies. What did I do on the weekends? Work on my business. Albeit the 'fun work' that I enjoyed most. But still work. What did I do in the evenings? Work. I had nothing beyond Grow Disrupt and the sales training practice I was in the midst of shutting down.

That was one of the most depressing realizations I'd had in a while.
I'd built my business in a bit of a whirlwind since 2014 and while I was

hardly impressed at the time, when I look back, I realize what I pulled off was substantial. I replaced my full-time income in under five months to walk away from my corporate job. A year and a half later, the sales training practice that was my ticket to freedom was one of the largest and most active headquartered in Central Texas. Then in mid-2016, I realized I didn't love being a sales trainer. It took me a lot of soul-searching to figure out what I wanted to do instead. I found a niche in producing "Grow Your Business" events *my* way. That meant no pitches, intimate settings, speaker access, and application-focused. We'd rebranded in 2018 but it was a process to shift how everyone knew me. Not to mention, events are challenging to make profitable even if you aren't handcuffing yourself by eliminating all the traditional money-makers (sponsors, speaker pitches, and post-event sales).

For months I'd been working exceptionally hard to juggle the sales training practice that kept the bills paid, launching Grow Disrupt, and trying to reclaim my evenings and weekends. To be fair, I *was* starting to reclaim most of my time off (minus short stints of intense project work). However, I quickly discovered that I didn't have much to fill evenings and weekends with so I ended up working anyhow. Again, I only allowed myself to do the "fun work" that I enjoyed. But it was still work. That night, I was too tired. I wanted a hobby that would be creative and fun and have nothing to do with my business. Some random neuron fired in my head and reminded me that there was still a violin shoved back behind the chaise-lounge by my bed. That sounded like fun, but I was a little embarrassed by my playing and didn't want my husband to hear me (after-all, it had been at least seven years since I last picked up the instrument!). So I went back to the bedroom, grabbed my headphones and that little electric violin, locked myself in my closet where the clothes could muffle the tiny sound and played.
For about fifteen minutes at least.

Armed with a few years of listening to really good violin playing, I quickly realized that I was not the violin prodigy I originally thought myself to be. It was Susannah, my younger sister and the totally non-nepotistic technology director for Grow Disrupt[3] who connected me with an instructor she knew in Dallas who was willing to give virtual lessons a try via Zoom (We were cutting edge at the time!). About six months later I realized that, although violinists laugh at the joke "it takes five minutes to learn how to play the violin, and five years to make it sound good," we are laughing because we know it's true.

---

3 That sounds sarcastic…but it's true! She's talented AF! I feel lucky to have her working with me!

This is the part where I relate this to Marketing, so now's the time to pull your ADHD brain back to attention!

When I started taking the violin seriously, there was one major aspect that both enthralled and frustrated me, especially as the virtuosos made the whole thing look effortless. That is, the violin is 100% transparent with the listener! It is a beautiful instrument, but it is also incredibly sensitive. Because of the nature of the violin, it amplifies everything the violinist does, both the good and the bad. It allows no lies. If the violinist is nervous, rushed, frustrated, or anxious, even an inexperienced listener can tell. If the violinist misses a note, a beat, or is off on the finger placement by a fraction of a hairbreadth, the violin will communicate that information to the audience with as much clarity as it communicates the violinist's passion and emotion.

It's that element of the violin that makes it so incredibly beautiful to listen to. It's that element of the violin that draws the listener in and lets them feel what the violinist is feeling without words to clutter things up. It's what makes violin music transcendent and impactful. But it's also part of what makes the violin so incredibly difficult to play well. It was the part that made it hardest for me to grow when, as a new violinist, I struggled just to play Perpetual Motion from Suzuku Book 1. It was hard for me to come to terms with the realization that it literally takes years to learn the foundations necessary to create music that sparks emotion and speaks effortlessly. Foundations that are learned bit-by-painful-bit. Learned by pushing through the awkward phases and the ugly songs that have no musicality and that no one wants to listen to. Most importantly, that every virtuoso went through the same thing.

This is the same reason MOST small business owners struggle in marketing as well.

Now that I look back through my 20-20 hindsight, I realize that I had the same problems and tendencies causing problems for me in my musical journey as early as my time in Alaska. I watched prodigies playing so beautifully and they made it look so natural that I berated myself for *not* being able to play and perform at that same level. Worse, I didn't realize that the awkward, frustrating part is how those virtuosos *got* to that success. I think part of this stems from the fact that I've always been pretty good at whatever I put my hand to. At some point as a child, I stopped realizing that I worked exceptionally hard for that success and just saw the success. When I picked up a task, a project or a hobby and failed to thrive instantly, I saw it as a personal failing. In high school and college,

I had straight As, and a lot of started-but-not-finished projects and hobbies. I'm sure the undiagnosed ADHD didn't help, but in my mind, as long as I quit the hobby before I discovered I wasn't good at it, I didn't fail, I chose to not compete.

Learning the violin was different though because I really *wanted* to be good at it, and I needed the outlet. So I persevered through the frustration and challenges. I sat and practiced scales and "drawing rainbows" with my bow for hours on end. I gritted my teeth at the challenge of making it sound anything like the recordings I listened to and kept practicing. I pushed through the aches in my arms and the torture of listening to recordings of myself that sounded dishearteningly far from Hilary Hahn or Lindsey Stirling. I fought to make the bow and my fingers move in concert and to learn where exactly those fingers needed to go. I struggled with trying to get my left hand, wrist, elbow, and arm all moving the right way and places at the same time I had to get my right hand and wrist and arm moving. The constant reminders (both in my head and from my instructor) to relax and remember to breathe didn't help. How often has it ever helped you relax when you're being told to relax? Maybe while the massage therapist is drawing out the tension with skilled hands. Every other time, it seems like it does the opposite! It was overwhelming and when I looked at others who made it look easy, all I saw was my inadequacies and their capabilities.

I've learned to look at those same performers with new eyes. To realize that even if their current practice sounds spectacular, and nothing like mine, they started here too. And the relaxed, effortless draw of the bow across the strings comes with practice.

I share this because it's so easy to find ourselves in the same position as business owners that I was as a violinist. As I share stories and ideas in this book, they may look like they were effortlessly creative but I want to encourage you to remember that it's the same scenario. These are marketing strategies and ideas that might have been spawned in a moment of brilliance or insight, but it was years of developing that marketing muscle and creativity that set up that moment of brilliance. And to be fair, more often than not, the brilliant part of that marketing started with a less than brilliant initial idea that was cultivated and elevated over multiple iterations.

I've always been interested in marketing, but understanding how it works and being able to market and sell out events during a global pandemic is the outcome of years of educating myself. More importantly, years of pushing myself to do the uncomfortable things. It looks easy because I have spent many long hours sitting at a computer trying to understand marketing analytics or brainstorming how to stand out and get attention for a client or an event. It's similar to watching a virtuoso on stage. However effortless it looks, it's only because I've spent thousands and thousands of hours focused on marketing at this point, both on the strategy side and on the execution side. Most small business owners dedicate less than five hours per week to marketing and almost none of that is on strategy.

 So here is my recommendation. Read this book and look for one aspect to implement.

Perhaps even stop when you find something you want to implement. Mark your spot, go implement that, then come back for more! Keep this book on your desk. Let the cover get tattered and worn as you work through it again and again. Take your time, get comfortable with the first idea and it will stretch your comfort zone and create growth. Then the next one won't be nearly so hard!

More than anything, do not let this book just become another book on the shelf full of ideas that were never implemented. Because marketing, great marketing, looks effortless as it changes the world. And that skill takes time to develop, But your business deserves the opportunity for your clients to know about you!

And please take advantage of the online community I've linked to at MarketingBeyondSocialMedia.com. Come on in and remind me how hard it is and ask for help breaking it down into the tiny steps that make sense for you! That's what it's here for! Because the reality is, for one last quick violin allegory, I came into learning the violin already knowing quite a bit about how to read sheet music. So even comparing my violin journey, no matter how slow it felt in the moment, to someone else's, is a recipe for disappointment no matter how you slice it. I also learned as an adult, knowing my learning style. It took a long time, but I learned to stop comparing my playing to Hilary Hahn or Lindsey Stirling.

And I'm happier and progressing faster because of it.

We are all on different journeys with different starting points but give yourself some grace because the same success awaits you in marketing!

The next section is going to dig into the biggest key that has allowed me to create massive marketing impact, on a shoestring budget, but if you're eager for more practical tactics:

1.

If you want the to find out why Social Media alone isn't working for you, skip to **Page 39**

2.

If you want to get straight to the meat and potatoes of how to market on a budget and come back to the rest later, skip to **Page 53**

Marketing Craves Creativity but Demands Investment!

When I was starting my career as a public figure, I always wanted to have some pithy, catchphrase that would stick in everyone's mind. If you've seen the episode of American Dad where Francine attempts to invent a catchphrase, you glimpsed how challenging that can be to land on inauthentically. Throughout the episode, she tries a bunch of different one-liners. Even going so far as to create branded swag with a couple. They all fall flat until the very end of the episode. I'm fairly sure the only reason the last one sticks is because the episode needed to end.

I had not seen that episode when I first started my business, nor do I think I would have even recognized to apply that situation, played up for humor, to my real life. But after months of trying to come up with something incredible and poignant, I let it go and just kept talking about marketing and the impact it creates. The more I talked, the more business owners I ran into that either wanted to just throw money at the problem to resolve it, or talk about how much they needed marketing, but did very little actual work on marketing their business. Over time I found myself repeating again and again, "Marketing craves creativity, but demands investment!" While "Marketing craves creativity" has become something of a catchphrase for me by now, I often find myself having to explain what I mean by, "Demands investment." Primarily because I'm not just talking about money.

Side note: This 'introductory story' to this concept highlights a takeaway that has been critically important to my whole life.

Namely: Stop searching for the 'perfect' anything. The perfect flier, the perfect email, the perfect landing page. There are no silver bullets in marketing. There are no silver bullets in anything to be fair. But you are never going to create the perfect tagline, the perfect funnel, the perfect graphic, the perfect ad that is going to drive sales instantly. It doesn't matter how long you agonize over getting that post out perfectly, it's not going to be perfect and it's not going to be the silver bullet that will save your business. I can't tell you the number of small business owners I've worked with who have spiraled into trying to find the perfect tagline. We'll talk about this more when we get to The 3 Ms, but understand, for now, this applies for you too! You're not going to find the perfect catchphrase or tagline by agonizing over it. You will find it when you're out there, talking to people and creating content and messages to distribute! Don't wait for things to be perfect, just get going.

Now, back to our regularly scheduled programming!

So what exactly do I mean by "Marketing demands investment." As we've already discussed, money is not our greatest asset. Both time and energy are more valuable resources than money and, as such, they can both be invested into marketing to produce a return on that investment. I often find that, because they are the more valuable resources of the three, when they are properly invested, they produce a higher return. Time and energy can be spent on creating strategies, analyzing results, and yes, designing and distributing marketing messages. If money is not as readily available, more investment of time and energy is needed instead to craft, distribute, and analyze evocative marketing messages.

Since neither time nor energy is boundless, smart business owners will focus on getting one tactic up and running well, then automate or outsource and start establishing the next one. Once a tactic is running relatively smoothly, business owners can then put energy and effort into doing the same thing with the next tactic. But putting no energy or time into your marketing because you don't have time to do everything you want is a recipe for disaster. Likewise, so is kicking off too many tactics at once and having no time to manage quality control.

In case you're wondering: yes, you can invest time without investing energy, but you will miss out on the compound interest effect that happens when you bring both. This is why I teach marketing beyond social media. Because for some people, social media marketing is energizing. For most people, it's exhausting and it's all they are told to do if they have a small budget. Which means that time may be going in, but not energy. That in turn is not attracting people to their business. If that's you, the lessons in this book and the 3 Ms of Marketing framework will help you find other marketing to do that *does* energize and excite you so you can invest both time and energy. If it's not you and you love social media marketing and content creation, It will give you the tools to exponentially improve your return on the time and energy invested there.

And for those of you wondering what to do if you have neither money NOR time…
I hate to break it to you but unless you get some stuff off your plate to free up time to work on marketing, your business is heading for closure. No one will market your business like you. Especially if you don't have money to pay for the really clever, creative, and experienced individuals to bend their brains towards your business. While you may want to hire someone to help you identify and fine-tune your messaging or distribute that message, you will want to be actively involved in the marketing for at least a little while. At the very least, you can participate in brainstorming content and getting photography and videos to be distributed through your marketing platforms. Clear some stuff off your plate. Make this a priority. Or one day, you will find yourself wishing you had.

The good news is that designing and distributing marketing messages is a wide variety of activities. It can be designing social media content and/or posting it. It can be designing or reviewing posters or fliers or mailers. It could be getting them ready for mailing and taking them to the post office. Even distributing them around the neighborhood yourself counts. It can be coming up with lists of media contacts, then investing time to build relationships with them to earn free PR opportunities. It can be attending educational conferences or implementing what was just taught (quick note: you're wasting your investment if you aren't making it to the application step!). It can be designing, then filming/recording commercials, or reviewing potential vendors. It could be reviewing marketing results at regular intervals. It could be baking bread or cookies to send to your clients or prospects. It could also be the time you take to sit down and brainstorm new tactics to implement.

Basically, the activities you're currently doing to spread the word about your business, even to put the business back in front of current clients, counts as marketing message distribution. And it's important, but it's the last M in the 3Ms of Marketing that I teach, for good reason! More on that soon…

On the one hand, hopefully this is exciting for you. It means you probably *are* investing time in marketing your business regularly. In the interest of helping you avoid the most common mistakes here and wasting energy, let's explore two pitfalls that frequently entrap today's small business owner:
How *much* time is being invested in marketing the business weekly
How much *energy* is being invested in marketing the business weekly

Time is easier to address and here's my challenge for you: For the next four weeks, log how much time you spend on marketing for your business.

If you have a timeclock system, you could go so far as setting up a "marketing" employee where you clock in and out while marketing your business. If you do this, consider yourself warned in advance to avoid the trap of letting yourself get pulled into multi-tasking and spiraling from one task to the next without remembering to clock out. Doing this will artificially inflate your time and give you a false sense of confidence. No. Your job is to log only the time actually spent designing that social media post, or crafting marketing messages, or passing out fliers to the neighboring homes after you finish a service to a customer.

In lieu of a timeclock, an excel spreadsheet designed in the following way may serve beautifully:

Date	Activity	Start Time	End Time

A printable version of this sheet is available for download at Marketingbeyondsocialmedia.com (literally, it's a one-button-click-to-download – no email necessary. This was made to be easy!). As an alternate option, at time of writing, I'm currently using a free app[4]. I love it! The one I use fills my brain's needs for bright colors and simplicity. There are lots of them out there. If you prefer to go digital and don't have an existing time-tracking program, find an app that works for you, is *easy*, and run with it. But do *not* let yourself spiral into trying to find the perfect app and fall into the trap of putting this exercise off indefinitely. If you can't land on an app in under five minutes, use the spreadsheet. Remember, there are no silver bullets, even for apps.

Set up your app or download the sheet, print off a few copies, and faithfully log your time for four weeks. Then add it up. How many hours are you averaging on marketing your business each week? If you're unhappy with the answer, what can you take off your plate to free up time to market your business? Could you automate tasks or hire an assistant to free you up? Putting in minimal hours long-term is not feasible, and this is not a negotiation. Not if you want your business to grow. Focus on the goal ("free up my time to focus on marketing") and a solution will appear!

_____

4 Because apps change as they update, I'm listing my current favorite time tracking app at.MarketingBeyondSocialMedia.com

If you're putting plenty of hours into marketing your business, and still not thrilled with the results, or looking to accelerate them, this next part is for you. But I get that not everyone needs this next section, so take the quiz below to identify if you should read the next section or skip it!

1. On a scale of 1 - 10 with 1 being "the bare minimum - it's a drain" and 10 being a raging "I F'N LOVE WHAT I'M DOING!", how much energy are you putting into marketing your business?

2. On a scale of 1 – 10, what percentage of the time you dedicate to marketing weekly or monthly is spent brainstorming fun and unique ways to distribute your message? (1=10% or less. Each added point adds 10%)

3. On a scale of 1 – 10, assuming you're holding these brainstorm sessions regularly, are you excited when you finish brainstorming?

4. On a scale of 1 – 10 (1 being 10% and 10 being 100%) what percentage of the marketing activities that you're executing get you excited?

> **If your answers add up to < 32, this next section is going to help you a lot, so keep reading!**

> **If it was 32+, you can skip to Page 39**

(Side note: If you're outsourcing your marketing and weren't able to answer the above questions because you're not involved, but you're definitely unhappy with the results, keep reading! You need this next part.)

Still here?

Awesome! Let's create some energy for your marketing because, as mentioned before, when your marketing activity is causing a neutral or drained reaction from you, it's not going to energize your prospects either. Prospective customers who are not energized and enthused by your marketing will not buy from you. That only exacerbates the situation. To either skip or break the cycle, we need to understand where it starts.

In my experience, it's almost always triggered by some combination of the three following problems:

1. We don't love our marketing message.
2. We really hate some of the tactics we feel forced to execute.
3. We aren't getting results.

Across hundreds of conversations about how much people hate marketing their business, #3 is almost always present in some capacity so we're going to start there.

I usually see this cycle start because small business owners are so frequently pulled by so many other urgent aspects of their business that they have nothing *left* to put into their marketing. Which means they put in the bare minimum possible to get their inner selves to shut up. Which, I understand. Marketing is often important, but not urgent. In some situations, marketing is just another thing to check off the list. They know they need to, so they "get it done," but it's kind of like spring cleaning as a kid.

I have a friend who actually looks forward to spring cleaning her house every year. I kind of get it now, but as a kid, it was the worst weekend of the year. My dad was a military man, so once a year, he would look up at dinner (usually on a Friday) and announce that we needed to cancel any plans we had for the weekend. It was time for spring cleaning. We would all grumble and cancel any plans with friends (or try and Tom Sawyer them into coming over and helping), then spend the next day deep cleaning the house and yard. None of us kids loved it. None of us looked forward to it. It was the equivalent of eating over-cooked, under-salted, limp and brown broccoli before getting a slice of chocolate cake. We got it done as quickly as possible and hoped we'd would have enough time to play with our friends afterwards. I guarantee, without Dad to spearhead and hold us accountable, it would have never gotten done.

Unfortunately, not many of us have a dad-like figure looking over our shoulders in business to ensure marketing is done. Which usually leads to:

1. Not enough marketing is going out
2. The small amounts that *are,* are not attractive to prospective customers

And when marketing that's going out isn't consistent, connected, and energized, it's a waste of energy to create it.

Now we're in the throes of the spiral. Marketing sucks to do because we aren't getting results. So we aren't doing much marketing and none of it is great. So we are getting fewer results. Now we're in the danger zone. At this point, even thinking about marketing is an energy suck. Making myself do something that isn't producing results just makes me feel like a failure. I'm not a fan of that feeling, so I start finding all kinds of excuses to avoid doing that thing. When small business owners start avoiding marketing for the same reason, **it doesn't help fix the situation**.

Some solopreneurs or very small business owners will hire a coach to hold themselves accountable to keep doing marketing. But this rarely addresses the root cause: they are not energized by their marketing.

The business owner who can afford it often chooses to outsource instead. They look for a marketing agency or firm that appears to get excited about marketing their business. The business owner hires them with hopes that the agency will bring the energy that the small business owner doesn't have to spare. The business owner is usually fairly engaged for a few weeks, but also tries to let the agency do their thing. The owner doesn't always speak up when something doesn't feel quite on-brand or make sense, convincing themselves that the agency knows best. Conveniently forgetting that the *business owner* is the one who knows the brand and market best. As soon as possible, the owner starts going hands-off. This is usually encouraged by the agency because then they can run unimpeded. Results in these situations, with minimal real and ongoing input to the agency from the person who knows the business best (the business owner), are almost always lacking.

That's, frankly, discouraging. If you're in this position (have hired, or are looking to hire an agency), keep reading. This next section is to help you know what to avoid so you can set that relationship up for success. If you're not looking to outsource your marketing and there is no burning curiosity to learn more on this line of thinking, you're welcome to skip to the **BOLDED HEADER**.

Why This Happens:

In most situations I've been privy to, once the firm is hired, small business owners almost entirely abdicate input and control until three to six months in, at which point the financial pinch is real. This often happens because, as mentioned, the agency tells the owner: "We know marketing! Let us do what we do best." And the owner, grateful to check the item off their list, leaves the marketing alone beyond a few initial interviews and goes back to paying attention to the fifteen other job descriptions they carry. Often consoling themselves that, "Marketing takes time and I've got six months of financial runway for this to take off!" In these situations, there are usually a lot of initial meetings where the owner does their best to communicate a living brand to the agency. Then the owner starts signing off on pretty much everything that gets sent over with the assumption that the agency understands the brand now and knows best.

Then six months in, the financial situation becomes tense, and results are still nebulous.

At this point, the owner is frustrated. That frustration tends to get reciprocated by the agency who now feels they were trapped because the owner starts bringing up all the things they didn't love, but signed off on because they thought the agency knew best. At this point, the owner usually starts getting more involved, cutting strategies that don't seem to be doing anything, and overall micro-managing to salvage their investment. Now the owner is frustrated, the agency is frustrated, and the relationship spirals from there. I haven't seen many of those situations redeemed.

I believe that, on top of very few people understanding the authentic nature of your brand or how to show-don't-tell your messaging, very few people will get truly creative about how to market your business. In many situations, they rely on safe content, basic and "proven" strategies, and a "hope and a prayer." This isn't usually done out of any malicious intent. The truth is that it's hard to get beyond that for a marketer juggling fifteen to twenty other brands at once plus their own. The ones that do, aren't affordable for most small businesses.

Without that intimate knowledge however, it's hard to get truly creative in a way that works for your business. But few people are as deeply entrenched in the business as you are. No one else is seeing the stories you are day-to-day from your clients. No one else is negotiating with vendors over key points to keep costs under control because you understand how quickly expenses can balloon. Rarely will a marketing team be able to speak to your business with the same eloquence as you do because they will rarely have the same level of passion as you do. But relying on "tried and true" marketing methods rather than digging deep into how to creatively present the brand in your marketplace is just a formula for wasted money and energy. On occasion you find someone who gets the industry, pays attention to what you're up to, and is creative. When that happens, it's because they have intentionally cultivated the creative marketing muscle. But it's not common and it's rarely cheap.

It's a hard line to draw here because, the right agency can actually both come up with creative messaging based on the communicated brand and put together some really creative ways to distribute that message. Most don't. Especially not for a small business budget. And even when you find a great agency that gets the brand and can craft a creative message, the business owner still needs to be involved in a focused quality-control approach as well as being proactive in regard to results tracking and communication.

In most situations, the business owner will need to be actively involved in coming up with how to execute the tactics and ensuring that whatever messages are put together to be distributed meet the brand's vibe-check. I'm all for the agency being part of a brainstorming session to "juj" up the message or come up with new tactics to distribute that message. As long as the business owner is involved in some variety of quality-control here.

If you skipped ahead, start reading again here!

Ok, so we've now established why most small business owners aren't energized by their marketing, whether it's in-house or out, let's talk about how to breathe a little life and energy back into your marketing!

The first place to check is your messaging. While we'll talk about this a lot more in the corresponding chapter, let's do some brief diagnostics. Answer the following questions as honestly as you can:

How many other people do you know that are using the same or similar message?

If your message *is* unique, is it because you're cramming more offers and solutions in than anyone else (e.g. coaching and massage therapy and laundry service)?

If you took the name of your business out of your message, could someone else use the same message without a problem?

What about your message do you love?

If you're not sure how to answer the above questions right off the bat, there's a solid likelihood that your message is part of the energy suck here. Remember how excited you were about your business before you got into the muck and mire of actually running all the details of your business? Before you learned the real ins and outs of your overly crowded industry? That's how excited you should be about spreading the word about your business. If you aren't, that's a problem! The good news is, if you keep reading, the messaging chapter should help you breathe some life into this soon!

Next up, it's always possible that you're trying to force yourself into a box with methods of distribution that you just don't love. For example, for years, I attended networking events.

Weekly.

I hated them.

I hated driving to them. I hated the name tags that never stayed on very well. I hated how the majority of the event was awkwardly standing on the fringes because I didn't already know people and everyone else was deeply engrossed in conversations with their best friends. I hated the endless and awkward sales pitches from poorly trained sales reps afterwards that I didn't know how to stop. I hated the emailing lists I found myself subscribed to because I gave them my card and they seemed to think that my email address being on the card was permission to add me to their list.

Basically, that was not a good marketing tactic for me. I dreaded it. And while I generated business from them, there are much better uses of my time, that generate a lot more business. I also know people who feel the exact same way about social media content creation. So now the question is, of the marketing tactics you're doing, what's making you want to pull your hair out? What do you legitimately hate doing?

It might be time to say goodbye to those tactics.

If you feel they are critically important to keep executing, it may be time to narrow down what portions drive you nuts and see if you can outsource those portions to an assistant (with detailed operating procedures to follow). Sometimes just changing our level of engagement can be enough to revive interest in a tactic that was previously driving you nuts. For example, when I stopped doing the graphic design and scheduling for our social media, I fell back in love with creating our social content.

If you are dreading *all* of your tactics, keep reading because adjusting your messaging might give you the motivation you need to enjoy the strategy before you throw it out the window entirely!

The last concept I'd like to touch on in this section on Greatest Lessons Learned in Marketing is the compound effect. We've all been shown the power of compound interest in terms of loans or retirement savings. If you haven't…here's a quick one to look at!

The Compound Effect

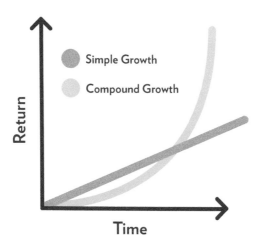

The compound effect is life changing because it creates something called Exponential Growth. An Exponential graph, if you remember from high school algebra, looks more like the line labeled Compound Growth on the graph above. It's one that appears to move very slowly at first and, in fact, may not appear to have any movement at all for a while. Over time though, it suddenly begins to show growth very, very quickly, rapidly surpassing the linear growth line.

As you may have guessed from the fact I'm bringing it up in a book about marketing, I've discovered that this is how marketing works as well.

Even if we *know* in our heads that linear growth doesn't happen in business, there's still a pervading belief that "if I add another marketing method, I should get that much more return." In other words, if I add one method of distribution, I should also move up one block on the chart regarding results. In this perspective, marketing results would grow linearly in response to marketing effort.

In my experience, it's just not true.

Marketing return grows exponentially. We add one marketing method and see a tiny bit of return. We add another and see a little bit more. We add another and see a little bit more. But at this point, we've usually been doing it all ourselves (or outsourcing without making sure we have time to keep quality control on-point) and we're stretched thin. We're either out of time, or out of money. So at this point, we start dropping strategies that don't appear to be producing much return. It's as much of a trap as continuing a method that is not producing *any* results at all once that method has had adequate time, revisions, and support to be effective.

Part of this happens because over time we build brand equity. Over time, the brand becomes more well recognized and therefore the messages we put out make a bigger impact. But marketing methods also require some time and energy to design and put into play, then to tweak until they are producing results. At that point, they must be streamlined and outsourced to free the business owner or marketing director to focus on another tactic while that tactic continues to run in the background with only quality-control input from the business owner. This way the old tactics continue to support the new tactics and *this* is what creates exponential return.

Smart business owners who are responsible for managing all of their own marketing will follow the process below:

1. Get the first round of marketing pushed out for the new tactic
2. Evaluate and adjust
3. Repeat steps 1 and 2 until key performance indicators (KPIs) are moving the right direction then...
4. Create a Standard Operating Procedure (SOP)
5. Hire someone else to do the repetitive work necessary for the tactic to be successful (This step might be more for my fellow ADHD readers than anyone else...)
6. Check in monthly to review KPIs and adjust proactively as needed.

This process allows us to continue adding tactics rather than having to swap them out. And if you've done the hard work of establishing how to make a tactic work, you can hire someone to execute at a reduced cost versus hiring an specialist[5]. Beyond bringing together marketing methods to establish space for exponential growth, there is also incredible power in bringing together time, energy, and money to produce a return on the investment. Now you understand why. Choose marketing tactics that energize you, that you're willing to put some time into, and maybe some money down the road and things invariably start growing.

---

5   To be fair – some things are just worth hiring a specialist for! The more complex and overwhelming a tactic is to kick off, the more likely it is that you'll want to hire a specialist. Don't disregard the need to manage the KPIs and quality control till they are moving the right direction however! Treat this with the same respect you would if you were kicking it off on your own.

The Psychology of Conversion Marketing

I imagine a Lion King-esque moment at this point in the book. Holding up this chapter and saying, with all the gravitas of Rafiki holding Simba before he ascends Pride Rock at the end of the Disney film, saying:

"It's time."

Mostly because studying *this* has been my true obsession for years. I figured if I could understand what happened in someone's brain when looking at marketing, I could increase the number of conversions too. But in the pursuit of that knowledge, I also learned that it's not just about understanding the psychology of conversions, so it was important to lay some groundwork first. Now that we're on the same page in regard to mindset and investments, let's dig into the practical aspect of crafting marketing that works for small business budgets. Let's talk about how marketing converts from a psychological level: Conversion Marketing.

One of the most important things to remember about conversion marketing is that the conversion doesn't usually happen from the initial brand exposure. Prospective customers don't convert just because they found you listed online, saw your billboard, heard your radio ad, met you at a networking event, read the right email, or saw the one perfect social post that went out yesterday. As I keep repeating: There are no silver bullets in marketing. Conversions happen when three things line up:

The consumer has trust with the brand.
They can and/or have envisioned what life is like on the other side of the purchase.

That vision sparks a release of dopamine and serotonin large enough to warrant the expense.

Sometimes we can target individuals who have already established #2 and #3 and try to just build trust so they choose to buy from us instead of from a competitor. This is usually the playground or the goal of legacy marketing like billboards, TV, radio, and print. As you might have picked up from that last sentence, this is always going to be an expensive path to choose. You will have to get your message out in front of a lot more people than if you are more strategic and can master the last two. Even if your goal is only to market to individuals who have established #2 and #3, we still have to build trust, so let's start there.

Trust with a brand can come from a couple of places. On the obvious side, long-term exposure to a brand that has performed consistently to brand expectations builds trust. We know when we go to McDonalds exactly what kind of hamburger, fries and drink we're going to get. They've performed to their brand image for years and most of us have seen them often enough over time to build trust. The reality is, whether it's a good burger or not doesn't matter. The brand is consistent and thus has established trust. It may not be a big enough dopamine rush, depending on your perspective, to warrant the purchase, but the trust is there.
This is the kind of trust that is built up after you've shown up in the marketplace as the Go-To provider for your industry for a long time. This is what happens when your brand is right there every time they look up something in that industry. This is what happens when every time they ask their colleagues or friends and family who to call, you're mentioned. It's what happens after they've been exposed to a consistent brand over time from multiple sources.

But we've all had an ad pop up on our social media feed that prompted a sale seemingly in an instant. The first time I remember this happening was when an ad appeared for a pair of blue light blocking glasses. They were on sale, but they were still substantially more expensive than I'd planned to spend that morning.
Yes somehow, fifteen minutes after seeing the ad, I got up off the couch, retrieved my wallet and input the credit card manually. For those of you who are familiar with conversion marketing, that's a pretty big feat. At that point in time, I had never seen that brand of glasses before. I certainly didn't wake up that morning planning to spend $90 on a pair of blue light blocking glasses and it's not like it was a negligible amount of money for me at the time. What happened?

There was an element of timing in this sale that was impeccable. My brother had come over the week before wearing glasses, which caught me off guard because I'd never seen him wear glasses before. When I brought it up, he mentioned that they were blue light blockers and how he'd noticed his eyes were less strained and he was able to get through the day in front of the computer without a headache ever since getting them. I was curious and filed it away while also wondering if perhaps the readers I was trying out to alleviate the headaches I got after staring at a computer screen all day weren't the answer. I hadn't consciously recognized that I should look up blue light blocking glasses yet, but they found me.

In the moment, it didn't register. But the graphic of the ad caught my eye. It was a classy looking businesswoman with a very stylish pair of glasses and some variety of text about blue light blocking. She was everything I wanted to be seen as early in my career as a small business owner. On top of that, the ad text spoke directly to me as a businesswoman. It was timely enough and felt relevant enough to me to get me to click to their website. I scrolled through the pages of designs till I found one I thought I liked but they were expensive and I wasn't sold yet. Then I saw a comment on the page about sharing your glasses to social media with their handle and thought I'd see if anyone had taken them up on that ask.

There were pages and pages of pictures on Instagram of every-day women who had shared their glasses from this brand sharing photos that highlighted the glasses. They were all posed over cups of coffee, working in beautiful locales, and looking quite studious, professional, and capable. I was intrigued. My brain reminded me of my conversation with Caleb, and I got myself up to make the purchase.

I hadn't even done any research to determine if they were any good at blue light blocking. I didn't feel I needed to. I saw hundreds of photos of women seeming to be extremely happy and it appeared that it would fit my lifestyle. I felt seen, heard, and understood. The timing was right. And I bought.

Obviously, I've seen hundreds if not thousands of ads on my newsfeed since. I've made decisions to buy in similar fashions, and I've also had many times where I've clicked an ad, visited their website, and left without a purchase. Almost worse, there are plenty of ads that I don't even remember seeing. So what's the difference? How do some companies succeed with advertising and marketing where others fail, even when they look identical? Since I'm telling this story in the section on building trust, I think it's fair to assume that that brand was able to build trust. Quickly.

They had testimonials throughout the website. Their graphics and photography were on-point, high quality, and showcased the brand in a way I could identify with. They had an easy-to-find and easy-to-read About Us section where I could learn about their CEO and her passion to support women professionals so they didn't have to settle for glasses built for men. I found testimonials online *easily*. Looking back, I think it's fair to realize that many of those testimonials posted on social media were paid posts by influencers. But in that moment, I didn't really care (And I still don't). There were a lot of people talking about the brand. I could see myself with them in my life, and I liked that vision.

One of the most important aspects of all this to note though is that, when I went to check-out, they had a PayPal option built in. For me, this not just made it easy for me to check-out (even though I had to update my credit card in my account), but it also reinforced that I could trust the checkout. I knew that, if I wasn't happy or they ended up being a scam, I could dispute it with PayPal and separately with my credit card company if needed. Interestingly, they had a slew of check-out options so I could pick the one I was most comfortable with. This isn't a commercial for PayPal necessarily. But this brand, that I didn't know, borrowed credibility from an established brand by having it as an option. You can do the same if you're in a similar world.

As we're all aware though, trust can't be forced. One of my biggest pet-peeves is a Testimonials page on a website. Identically annoying are the rotating banner of testimonials on the home page that show three testimonials with five stars. I just skip those sections, don't bother clicking on the page, and I know I'm not alone. None of us want to be 'sold' to! From a psychology perspective, pictures, videos, and embedded testimonials go markedly further. If you want an example of how testimonials are embedded throughout the website in a way that the viewer will easily read and absorb, but not necessarily notice, check out GrowDisrupt.com

Testimonials and graphics are not the only way to build trust. Since building trust is the cornerstone of sales, I'm a big fan of ensuring I'm leveraging every possible element that might come into play. The best analogy I ever came up with when I was running my sales training practice was, "Trust is like a piggy bank." Everything I do is either making deposits into or withdrawals from that piggy bank. Some of those withdrawals, I can't control! Someone is going to decide not to pick up this book or take me seriously because they were taken advantage of by a marketer with curly hair in the past, they don't like the cover, or think the opening to address ADHD is a gimmick and ADHD is an over diagnosed neurodivergency. There's literally nothing I can do about that!

My goal is to make sure that I've set up as many possible "deposits" through the cover design and at-a-glance layout as I can. I've done this in hopes that, at the end of the day, there are more deposits than withdrawals to support the right person in making a buying decision. Every time I am consistent or live up to expectations or show someone I understand them in how I've laid out my marketing, I make deposits into the trust bank.

One really great way to facilitate trust is through leveraging Stage Selling.

To be clear, I'm not talking about the silly game that some influencers play where they first try and convince you to buy a $99 product, then a $30 add-on, then a $299 secondary purchase, etc. I'm not a fan of those (often) click-bait based funnels that usually lead to buyer's remorse. What I am a fan of is recognizing that sales happen in stages. If I want to convince someone to part with money, I'm going to need to focus on **winning each individual stage of the sale because each time I do, I make deposits into the piggy bank of trust.**

Before we can do that though, it's important to for us to be on the same page about what I mean when I use the word "sale."

My definition of a sale, again from my sales trainer days, is the exchange of value between two individuals. That's it. It's basic. It's easy to remember. It's simply the exchange of value. This could be me giving someone a ticket to our events where they will get information and energy and support that is valuable to them. In exchange, they give me money. But, in a simpler sense, this could also be me giving them value in exchange for their time.

Remember though, we've already established that value can be money, time or energy/attention! When we start to realize that we, as the seller, must provide value in exchange for someone's energy or attention, and even the smallest fragment of their time, we start to grasp the power of stage selling.

In practical terms, this means that getting someone's attention (energy) is the first sale. If I live up to expectations and they feel that giving me their attention was worth it, then they will usually move to the next stage, which is taking time to actually absorb the content of the ad. What does that mean in practical terms? The graphics or "hook"[6] get the attention. If the rest of the ad lives up, they will give me enough attention to read the ad itself. If that lives up they'll move to the next stage. Prospective customers check out of the process when they do not feel like they were given enough value in exchange for their investment. Every time.

One of the easiest ways to provide value is to spark emotion in your viewer. Unfortunately, most small business owners focus first on trying to provide value in terms of knowledge first. To an extent, I get it. We are conditioned to pay for knowledge from paying for university to paying for news services and continuing education classes and events. There is an inherent belief that knowledge is valuable. But we often overlook the realization that, for that knowledge to be valuable, it must be desired knowledge. I'm guilty of this as well. There have been plenty of times that I've attempted to foist education on my audience, not realizing that they had little interest in that information.

The good news is, we also highly value something else. Something much easier to spark in your audience: emotions. The Taylor Swift Era's tour that swept the globe is a phenomenal example of this. It was more than a billion dollars of people paying to experience the emotion of the concert live (and the movie afterwards). An incredible amount of overpriced merch was bought not for the quality, but solely to be able to relive that emotion at-will. We pay to be amused. We pay to be entertained. We pay for emotions and the most powerful emotion we can spark in our marketing to create a conversion to the next step is always curiosity. Because curiosity causes an itch that can only be put out through acquiring knowledge. If you want to educate your audience, you must first help them be curious. Spark curiosity with your marketing and you'll be amazing at how much further it will go.

If I've provided enough value in exchange for getting their attention and the time it's taken them to absorb my marketing, then following the Call To Action is usually a no brainer. There are a couple of calls to action that we might use here to draw them closer to the sales portion of your conversion process. Since how they interact with your brand all the way up till they get into the sales conversation is still a great opportunity to reinforce your message through marketing, let's talk about it!

To be clear, there are probably a few more calls to actions you could use in your marketing than the two I'm about to explore in more detail. You might have ads whose whole role is just to convince someone to submit their

---

6 A hook is the first line of ad copy. This could be the headline. This could be the first line of a radio ad or TV ad. It could be the text inside a graphic on a social media ad. It could be opening line of the text in the actual ad copy itself.

contact information. You might have ads whose whole goal is just to get people to book appointments immediately just from the ad. I will be super straight that I think that the second one is usually a mistake. The people who will book a sales appointment with you from an ad are usually too cold. You'll still need a warm-them-up process between the time they book and the appointment itself. You could send them to your website, or create an automated series of emails to introduce them to your brand, but you'll need to do something to keep drawing them in. In most situations, even if they submit their contact info first or book an appointment, you'll still want to draw them to your website for further exploration. So let's start there.

If your goal is to get them to your website:
In digital marketing and printed marketing, the next goal is typically to get them to visit the website, either by scanning a QR code, clicking a link, or actually typing it into their browser. If I have done a good job providing value in exchange for their attention first and then again for their time, this next step usually isn't too hard. The most important thing to recognize about this next step is that, before my content on my website can do the selling on my behalf and answer whatever questions they have, I have to keep them engaged enough to read what I've put there.

They will first glance at the overall design of the page. If they start to feel overwhelmed or don't easily see prompts to guide them to the answers they are looking for (whether they are aware of those questions or not), I will lose them. In essence, my branding and designs need to support the promises I've made through my previous ad elements. For starters, my graphics can't feel so disparate from the ad that the visitor feels like they are on a different website. My brand needs to feel cohesive and subconsciously support the message that I'm providing. For example, my marketing message is all about creativity and getting attention. So my brand, in this book and on my website (TheStephanieScheller. com if you want to check it out!) is artistically inspired, and brightly colored! The brand we built for GrowDisrupt.com is all about helping our event guests break through to the next level in their business, so we use breaking glass and warm, bright colors offset with strong, stable colors that feel luxurious as well.

As long as the brand is strong and cohesive, now I can focus on pictures, videos and testimonials that give my prospective buyer a glimpse of what it is like to have the purchase as part of their life. I am still in awe of how beautifully that blue light blocker company threaded suggestions throughout the website to post online with their hashtag so it was easy for me to go look at that when I was ready. It was more persuasive than a testimonials page that I never would have cared to click to. One thing that is too often overlooked in today's buying climate is the importance of the About page on the website. Our buying economy wants to know that they are buying from the right company who is a trusted expert and whose values align with theirs. This is often a section that is frequently under-emphasized and left overly generic and bland. That's wasted marketing space! This should, as much as anything else on the website, help drive home your marketing message.

I also recommend ensuring that frequently asked questions (FAQs) and professional pictures are prominently featured. We'll talk about getting your website all in line later, so for now, just know that if you're driving people to the website, you'll want to make sure it's intuitive for them to get their questions answered and feel confident that you're a legitimate brand. Your FAQs may live on their own page that is featured in the menu (like at TheGrowRetreat.com) or may exist on each individual page if you're selling a handful of things and want those answers readily available to the buyer. Professional, custom pictures go a long way to reassuring your prospective customer that you're a legitimate company in today's age of internet fronts.

If all of that is in place properly, the last step to check is the Call To Action. Usually an invite to either check-out or fill out a form (book an appointment or request more info). Whatever your Call To Action, it has to be exceptionally clear, and easy for them to follow. It should load quickly when they click. I can't tell you how many times I've clicked to check-out and then got stuck in a 10-12 second loading hell. That seems small but if their website can't handle my request to follow the Call To Action, it's enough to make me question their ability to fulfill on the purchase.

A QUICK CHECKLIST TO CHECK YOUR WEBSITE:

1. Look first at overall aesthetics. Where is your eye drawn to? If you look at the site through squinted eyes, what does the brand tell you about this company? Do you know what to read first, second, and third or are there a lot of things competing for your attention?

2. Un-squint your eyes and look at the details. Is the text broken up by professional looking photos? Is the text easy to read?

3. Is it easy to absorb information I may be looking for

unconsciously (like info about the company or testimonials?)

4. Lastly, look for the call to action, is it easy to find and clear?

If you're looking to generate a call from your marketing:

First, let's recognize that in most situations, you will start by driving someone to your website, even if the end goal is a call. But if you're working with legacy marketing like billboards, TV, or radio, and your goal is to generate a call instead of a website visitor, you've still got some work to do here in terms of subconscious marketing to get them all the way to the sales process. And sometimes it's harder because if you are using legacy marketing, you probably have a team answering the phone and handling that next step for you. And this means, while you can establish a set of ground rules for your team to follow, it's the culture of your company that will make or break this next step.

Some great ground rules to start with:

1. Answer the phone within three rings – don't leave your prospect wondering if you're around

2. Answer the phone with a smile on your face and a pre-authorized script that helps support the marketing message (I.e. "[Name of company], how can I help you today?" versus "[Plumbing Company Name], home of the fairy godplumbers, how can I magic away your plumbing problems today?"

3. Listen closely! One of the biggest pet peeves in customer service is when someone listens to respond instead of understand. Listen and ask questions to ensure you understand what they are calling about before worrying about responding.

But all these rules are useless without a culture that supports it. You can buy mirrors for your customer service reps' desks to help them remember to smile, but if your culture is stressed and anxious and they don't want to smile, the prospect will feel the forced in-authenticity and it's not going to convert for you. If your marketing relies on a customer service rep to answer the phone and make the conversion, invest in making your culture match your message! That means taking time to run team meetings where you help them reconnect with the mission, message and core values. That means taking time to take care of your team. It requires time and energy and it's part of your marketing. Remember what I said earlier, your marketing is only as strong as the company it represents.

Overall:

The best buying situation is finding someone who has already established a need for the product and is looking for the best provider. In this sense, we get to enter the sales process halfway through and it saves a lot of time! At Grow Disrupt, that means finding someone who has already decided that they want to attend an event to help grow their business. This means, instead of trying to convince someone that they need to attend an event, I can focus on convincing them that we're the best option.

Note that I still have to get and hold their attention, but instead of having to first convince them that they need to buy an event ticket, then convince them to buy from me, I just focus on convincing them to buy from me.

As mentioned before however, this can get expensive. Unless you can identify the one or two things that your buyer does right as they are at the cusp of making a buying decision, you're going to have to get your messaging out in front of a lot of people to find those ready-buyers. As a rule of thumb, every pair of eyeballs you put your message in front of requires some variety of investment. And even then, there's no guarantee that you'll actually convert that individual because we, as buyers, tend to be more inclined to spending money with the company that was present through most of our consideration journey.

In other words, you will still need education-based marketing campaigns (like articles, PR, social media, etc) that spark curiosity and interest. You will still need nurture campaigns (like social media, email lists, outreach campaigns) to help bring green buyers all the way to the point of purchase. Mostly, you will still need to ensure that your website or customer service representative who answers the phone or greets them at the door, is equipped to handle their questions.

That's a lot of info so let's sum up a bit here!
1. Trust is crucial to generating sales (the ultimate goal of marketing).
2. We have to stop thinking about our advertising in terms of "How do I get people to buy?" or "How do I get people to visit the website or call?" and instead start thinking about "How do I get people to stop and actually pay attention to my ad?" It shifts our effort and our results. Instead of trying to cram enough info in to build trust right away, ask yourself what you can do that will get attention first. Then what can you do to be worthy of the attention they are giving you? The process builds from there!
3. Understand that even when you get them to the website, it's not about building out great content first. It's about understanding how to get someone to READ the content you produced and feel confident and comfortable with your brand both in terms of how the messaging is represented in text _and_ in design/graphics. Choose a brand that supports your messaging. Select graphics that help them envision life with the product. Make it easy for them

to get to the next page and the next, to absorb the testimonials, and to follow the Call To Action without hesitation or getting overwhelmed.

Action Item: Jesse Cole, owner of the Savannah Bananas and "The Yellow Tux Guy" has a saying that attention beats marketing every time. To GET attention, you've got to have something worth looking at. In my experience, that usually means something physical! His Yellow Tux stands out on the green baseball field. My violin sets me apart from most of the other keynote speakers in the US. Take a minute and jot down three tangible things that are quintessentially you that you can use to get people to pay attention to your marketing so you have the opportunity to build trust! Maybe it's a haircut? A specific hat? A t-shirt? Vivid colors in your hair? A specific style of jewelry? Bagpipes? Get creative! And remember that you don't have to land on it perfectly today. Come up with something, and then if it's not getting attention or not working, do something else until you find the thing that does!

The 3Ms of Marketing:

I had an amazing psychology instructor in college (shoutout to Dr. Frey!) and I became obsessed with psychology and understanding the brain. One thing in particular that fascinated me was how psychologists put together studies to test theories and control variables. I participated in a couple of these studies for extra credit just in case I bombed the final. I was always intrigued at how hard the scientists worked to ensure that the variables were not responsible for affecting the outcomes. Without that control, it's hard to know if the knowledge gleaned is accurate. The risk that an inaccurate conclusion caused by a failure to control variables could mislead further theories and frameworks and create unreliability in the work being executed is real. If the variables are not controlled, the conclusions cannot be trusted. When I got into my first full-time job in 2011, I had the chance to run my own similar study, with controls on most of the variables, in regards to small business marketing.

At the end of my first year in sales for the media organization I worked for, I was asked to take the reins of the Retention department. I was reluctant at first, but looking back, I'm grateful I did. I worked in the digital marketing department. When I started working for that company, I sold SEO, SEM, SMM and a bunch of other annoying acronyms to small business owners who didn't know any better. As the Head of Retention, my job was to manage a small team and decrease the number of accounts that cancelled before they got to the end of their first year with the company. Out of the entire country, our location's sales reps had the lowest retention rates. As I was advised when I was asked to take over the department: "Less than 40% make it to three months, and less than 14% make it to a full year…and you're it." That shocked me. My accounts were the only ones making it to a full year and beyond? I'd barely been working there for a year. I only had a few accounts that were even old enough to make it to a year! But to be fair, most *were* making it to three and six and even nine months with no indicators that they were going to cancel.

I finally agreed, not realizing what I was getting myself into.

I got a crash course in marketing and management the day I took over. Prior to taking over, the team had pretty much run rogue. Driving home that day, I felt the weight of the world as I tried to figure out how the hell to fix the retention numbers and take care of this team without alienating anyone. The good news was, they were actually excited to have me spearhead and organize the department, but there were a lot of issues (not the least of which came from decisions my boss was making). I quickly realized that our current method of retention, calling clients back *after* they'd gotten frustrated and left us an angry voicemail or email wanting to cancel, was a terrible strategy. While we worked hard to triage the abandoned and angry accounts, we also worked hard on shifting the department from firefighting to garden-tending. That meant taking care of the accounts from the minute they were sold.

As soon as an account was sold, it was put on my desk to be assigned to someone on the retention team. That person's job was then to call and confirm that the strategy and goal the small business owner was hoping for lined up with the information put on the page by the sales rep. They rarely did and we made a lot of changes before paperwork was even submitted to the build-out team. But it worked. Within three months, our retention rate had increased to 86%. I was pretty damn proud.

More importantly, though I wouldn't realize it till months later, I had the opportunity to run some incredible studies on how marketing worked. The kinds of studies Dr. Frey would have been proud of. Namely: Because I got to assign out the new sales to members of the team and myself to manage, I became the control factor. When two landscaping companies came across my desk in the same week, with the same package, I assigned them to myself so I could test out what was working and what wasn't. I did the same thing with a kindergarten school, multiple niches of attorneys, a couple of bars, and a few others. What had always frustrated me about our program was that sometimes the $500/month SEO program would take off like lightning. Within months, the recipient would be getting 30-50 calls per month of solid leads.

Sometimes, it sputtered and barely moved. When we'd check in at the three-month mark, the account would have three phone calls. Total. One of them was a wrong number. One was their receptionist calling to see if the tracking phone number was working. One was their mother wondering why the business had a new phone number.

I saw it happen while I was a sales rep between my accounts and my coworkers, but I didn't have the sales volume or control to be able to run variable-free tests. Here, I was pretty sure I could eliminate the 50-50 shot at success. If I could do that and identify the markers to focus on during the build-out, I could train my team could do the same. I spent days in a thrill-induced haze, picturing a retention of 100% because all of our accounts were massively successful. I was going to produce *only* exceptional campaigns.

Spoiler alert.

I did not.

There were still campaigns that underperformed, and campaigns that performed like champs. Frustrated, but curious, I began looking beyond and I quickly realized that the difference between the underperformers and the overperformers was what I eventually coined the Three Ms of Marketing:

1. The Target Market
2. The Marketing Message
3. The Methods of Distribution

The campaigns that performed well did so because the owners knew who their ideal target market was, and had details. Not just demographics so they knew whether listings on our website would help them convert, but also psychographics so they could build the marketing information on that page to appeal to the end buyer.

Additionally, they had clarity on their marketing message and knew what they needed to communicate to resonate. They knew that their messaging went beyond a tagline and a snappy logo. They knew what they needed to show to help the viewer understand what made them special. And they showed it, not just in the text on the page, but in the graphics and videos too.

Lastly, they knew what methods they were using to distribute that message in a way that put it in front of their ideal buyer, and they made sure those methods worked together. The best performing campaigns were the ones where the owners went all in and used "See our listing on [Name of Website]" and "As Seen On [Name of Website]" elsewhere in their marketing. These were the people who used us as a trust-building factor in addition to the in-the-background work we were doing for search engine rankings. In other words, the work they hired us to do was supplemental to the other strategies that were running. Ringing any bells in relation to the chapter on Exponential Marketing?

I'm not going to pretend that if you have the 3 Ms of Marketing you can do any kind of marketing campaign and get results. You still need to be incredibly intentional about which methods you choose. But I am saying that the 3Ms of Marketing have repeatedly been the difference between a beautifully cooked porterhouse steak, and a thin and runny bowl of gruel when it comes to marketing results.

They are also the three things that will give your cohesive, comprehensive, exponential growth marketing plan some structure.

So let's dig in a little more to these.

The Target Market: What it is, Why Build It, And How to Build It

"I thought I knew my target market before we did this exercise. Now I realize I knew [so little] about [them]."
Susan Rossbach
CEO
Brains4Drones

I feel you, Susan!

What is a Target Market

Before we get going, I want to clarify. This is not another of those "You need to niche down" chapters. We've heard that before. And the way it's presented is usually full of blame and shame and rarely helpful. I do understand that a defined niche helps. Trust me! Life got a lot easier when we found our ADHD niche for Grow Disrupt. Mostly because a great niche makes you that much more memorable. It's hard to remember someone who can do anything for anyone when it's time to refer out a potential buyer. Beyond even that, you probably should have *some* idea of what makes your buyer special versus other buyers in your industry. We've all heard it before: when you try to market to everyone, you'll end up appealing to no one. But when I was getting going with my first small business, it took me a long time, a lot of trial and error, and a lot of clients, to figure out who was my ideal buyer. Much less to really understand what made them different from the rest. Despite starting the "Grow Your Business" events in 2017, it wasn't until 2021 when I was analyzing how we'd doubled in size during a pandemic when so many in my industry were barely even surviving that I discovered our ADHD niche. The amount of stress I could have avoided if someone had just told me to do my best to narrow it down a little bit, and then keep refining it as I continued growing would have been unbelievably helpful.

So let me be that person for you!

I personally have found that sometimes it is a matter of narrowing your focus to a primary target market to help structure your marketing message and methods. But beyond that, most small businesses are going to have secondary, tertiary and possibly quaternary target markets. My rule of thumb is that you're allowed to have as many target markets as you are willing to research. It's certainly easier to market if you *can* narrow it down to one specific, clearly defined target market. But if you're already agonizing and panicking over *another* chapter to make you feel bad for not having your target market figured out…take a breath, this isn't that and I'm not a "purist" here.

The last thing I'll say on this particular aspect is that, especially as a small business, it's not very likely when someone calls you up who is outside of your normal demographics and asks if they can give you money that you'll refuse as long as it's a reasonable request. Obviously, there are some scenarios where you *should* refuse. E.g. Mr. Shady calls you up and asks if they can launder money through your business in exchange for 1% of the take. But for the most part, especially as you're establishing yourself, if someone calls and wants to give you money for legal and ethical work that you're capable of doing, you're not going to tell them, "Sorry! My target market is women in their 30s with blue hair from Cleveland." You'll take the money and the work! And that's okay. The Target Market is an *internal* document. You're allowed to have clients who don't fit it perfectly, *especially* as you get started. But your marketing should speak clearly to your demographic. The target markets function as a guide to limit wasting your valuable marketing resources.

So let's talk about having multiple target markets!

Remember when I said that small business owners are allowed to have as many target markets as they want to take the time to build out? The key is that each individual target market must be narrowed down enough to have a *few* core identifying factors in both demographics and psychographics. I.e. your target market can be "men and women from mid 20s to early 40s" as long as you have some specific identifiers both in the demographics (physical details about their lives) but also in the psychographics (the mental details of how they think). Some good rules of thumb to keep in mind when deciding where the differentiators are:

1. Don't span more than one generation or a 15-year period

2. If you can't get identifying characteristics in both demographics and psychographics, narrow the age range, industries, or gender focus.
For example:
Not Defined:
People in the finance world who want to be top performers.
Defined:
Financial Advisors in their late 20s and 30s who live in Texas (demographics) and who want to be part of the Million Dollar Round Table (psychographics).

I'll just re-iterate one more time though that most of us will go through a few iterations and rounds of sales in our businesses to find our perfect target markets. I went through a *lot* of sales meetings to find out who wanted to buy from me and, more importantly, who I wanted to sell to. It took years of building personas and evaluating my target market to 'niche down' like I am now. The key is to start with some identifiers for now and constantly refine from here.

Before I get too far from that sentence, let's clarify the difference between a Target Market and a Buyer Persona. At least in my book. I'm a big believer in going back to the entomology of a word, or at least looking at definitions to try and figure out what something is. Most definitions I've found mark a Persona as a fictional character that exemplifies the target market. These are useful because it's easier to build marketing that feels personalized when you're marketing to "Kim, mother of four who loves Yoga and Frozen Yogurt!" than it is to market to "Women between the ages of 40 - 55. Hobbies: Yoga. Where Do They Shop: Frozen Yogurt Shops." But the latter is easier to identify *where* marketing needs to be placed. Personas help you develop the message that will resonate best. Target Markets help you put that message where they will see it and respond.

Another difference, Personas are often a page or two at most. The Target Market is going to be a lengthy document that lists out both the demographics and psychographics of your typical buyer. This will typically cover everything from their age range, job titles, industries, marriage status, gender identity (where applicable), family life, hobbies, and both online and offline hangouts. It will also look at what they love, what they hate, what they aspire to, and what drives them crazy. In my experience, these are typically eight to fourteen pages long and they are living, breathing documents. Yes, you'll do a bunch of research up front to fill out as much as you can. But then, you'll be editing.

And editing.

And editing.

Every time you learn more, you'll go in and adjust. You'll learn more as you work with clients that you realize you *hate*. For example, the day I added "is not a narcissist" to our psychographics was empowering. You'll learn more as you find the clients that you adore. You'll learn more as you move around in your world. That's okay. You're learning and growing.

WHY Build a Target Market

I'm optimistic that you probably don't need this next section, but it seems dangerous to just *not* add it to the book.

CRAFT YOUR COURSE

1.

If you're already convinced that you need detailed Target Markets but wondering where to go to get all that information (short of stalking and harassing your clients [this is a bad idea – just in case you couldn't tell]) – Skip to **Page 64**

2.

If you've already got that information collected, you can skip to **Page 70**

3.

If you're question-ing why on EARTH you would dedicate anywhere from 4-8 hours researching a multi-page document of stats on your ideal buyer...
keep reading.

A few years back Tom reached out to ask if I could put together a marketing plan for him. His product was straight forward and simple with no downside for property owners. In theory, he should have been making a lot more money than he was. His model placed a large metal bin, branded to advertise for passerby-ers to drop off old textiles that were too old to be donated, on high traffic properties. A sensor in the high-tech bin alerted his office whenever the bin was full and he'd deploy a worker to pick up the recycling so they could sell it for so many cents per pound. Whoever owned the property that the bin was placed on would then receive a portion of the revenue from that bin monthly. It was a solid system with a nationwide brand behind it. And Tom loved it because he had a real heart to support his local school districts as well. He already had some bins placed at a couple schools a little outside of his immediate area and any schools that gave him permission to place a bin could generate hundreds of dollars to help offset school fundraising efforts. By his calculations, if he could put a bin on each of the schools in his independent school district, he would be able to provide $87,000 per year in additional revenue to the school district. Not exactly chump change!

But none of them would return his calls or outreaches.

He'd been sending letters, calling, and even trying to drop by for months. He tried asking his current clients to refer him to other locations. They were avid fans of his, but because they were technically in another school district, it went nowhere.

So, my team and I dug into the research and planning.

Two weeks later when I sat down with Tom to go over the marketing plan we'd put together for him, I got past presenting the target market, the marketing message, and started with the method of distribution and he stopped me. I was recommending that he start the outreach process by sending a postcard to each of the schools and he was already shaking his head. They'd tried mailing letters to the schools in the past and he wasn't ready to waste more money on mailers. To be fair, I understood his position. That was one of a few times in my entire marketing career I've thought mailers made sense. I let him explain his resistance, then pointed out that I'd reviewed the letters he had been sending. The postcards we'd designed were very different. I showed him the design and laid out the psychology behind them. He wasn't sold.

So, I finally told him to give them a try. If he ran the process I'd put together and it didn't work, not only would I refund him the money he'd paid us to do this research, but I'd reimburse him for the mailers too. It was a hard offer to refuse. I completed the presentation, and he got the postcards printed and mailed. A week later, it was late one afternoon when my phone lit up with Tom's name. I picked it up to hear:

"What did you do?"

A little confused, I asked him to elaborate, and he went on to explain that the mailers started arriving that day. He already had three people call to ask, not whether he could come out to meet with them and present the process, but when he could place a bin on their properties.

Every time I tell this story, invariably, someone's hand goes up and they ask to see the postcard. But one of the reasons it works is because it's unique. I'm not going to undermine that. Besides, what works for someone else isn't guaranteed to work for you. One of the reasons I think the postcard worked so well is because Tom had spent so long putting his brand in front of them. Albeit in ways that didn't prompt action, but there was already some subconscious brand familiarity. When they received a well-designed Call To Action, it was easier to *take* action than it would have been otherwise.

That said, I will share what we *did* on the postcard that made it so effective, so the concepts can be implemented. First, we kept the card extremely simple. One large call to action on the front that was customized to each school plus one descriptive graphic. One short sentence with bullet points on the back and a QR code to learn more that led to a landing page of frequently asked questions.

In other words, we made each individual school feel special. The card was designed in a way to indicate that we understood their situation and known concerns both in the selected headlines and in how we avoided putting a burden on them with a huge block of text to read. We researched the information we knew they were being pushed to pay attention to by the superintendents, then put that front and centered, bolded when necessary.

How did we come to this?

We realized early in the research that Tom's ideal buyers were inundated with pitches. The office administrator went through the mail and tossed 99% of it before their boss would even see it. They were overworked, stressed as hell, and felt unseen in many ways. Putting the name of their school on the front made them feel seen. We also tapped into some of the pressure they were receiving from higher-ups regarding the need to implement more green recycling initiatives. And it translated to sales. Quickly. Target market research told me that the best way to get in front of these administrators was PTA meetings, finding the right bars, or mailers. Tom didn't have time to hang out at bars or attend PTA meetings, so as much as I typically hate mailers. We leaned on those. And it worked.

Later that same year, Dana gave me a call and she was equally frustrated. She'd been working *hard* to get in front of doctors for years. But doctors are notoriously difficult to contact. Pharmacy reps spoil them with lavish and endless lunches. Lunches that they rarely have time to eat. They are overworked and exhausted. And this was pre-pandemic! When Dana showed up with plates of goodies and fliers, it got lost in the crowd. Our market research once again showed us what we could already guess: they have an insane amount on their plates. Getting their attention is tough. It's hard to even have time for the stuff that they care about most, including living a healthy lifestyle. Also, the research reminded us that they know and hang out with other doctors. Based on this, we knew that if we could get in front of them the right way, we could probably get in front of more of them, *if they had something remarkable to talk about.*

Up till now, Dana had been sending mailers, drop-bys etc. She'd did great work and asked for referrals, but they were few and far between. It was simple, medical billing is rarely the thing doctors are discussing in their down time. If they are having trouble with the medical billing in their practice, they don't always feel comfortable admitting that to their colleagues, so opportunities for referrals were few and far between.

I recommended a more similar approach to what she *had* been trying, with one big difference. We designed a credit-card sized card and had a handful of them laminated. On the front of the card, text highlighted that Dana's goal was to be part of their team and support them. Then provided instructions for the doctor to receive a week of free healthy meal kits, once a month for three months as a gift from Dana. She didn't ask for any appointments, just offered to help them out. All they had to do was text her with what week they wanted their meal kit delivered to their office. The back of the card then provided instructions that, once they had redeemed this, they could pass the card along to another doctor who needed the same support.

Dana ended up having to, within a couple of months, ask the doctors to hold on to the cards and not pass them along anymore until she could get caught up. Over several years of business prior, she'd generated connections with at least a couple hundred doctors. Within three months, she'd created direct connections and relationships with sixty doctors. While she didn't ask for appointments to present her business solutions to them, by the second month of dropping off the boxes, she was being asked to come in and share what services she provided.

So!

I get it. Building a target market, the way I'm about to teach you, takes time. A lot of time. But it also drastically decreases the number of resources that end up being wasted in your marketing. Both in terms of money and in terms of energy. When you understand your target market, you can get in front of your ideal audience faster and you can design a marketing message that resonates more. This leads to faster conversions, at higher rates. And focusing your marketing methods means you'll waste less money and less energy.

The short of all this?

Detailed and defined target markets convert more clients, faster, with less money and maximize your time by allowing you to focus on methods that have a drastically higher likelihood of working.

How To Build a Target Market

For those who skipped ahead, cool! Obviously, that's the point of this book! But a quick word of warning: if you're reading this next section and thinking "This is crazy…I don't have time for this… Stephanie is insane. She has to understand that none of us can do this!" Do yourself a favor: go back and read the stories I just told. Because none of that is possible if you skip the coming step.

Trust me. I've done this enough times. I've run marketing plans, knowing about the 3Ms and thinking that, because I know them, because I invented them, I don't always have to follow them to the letter. Without a detailed and defined target market, even my team and I have a hard time coming up with anything truly creative that actually works like the stories I've talked about.

Ready?

Let's dig in to how to build a Target Market. Starting with what information composes a target market. These are all the items that we research on every single target market, both the demographics and the psychographics:

Demographics:
- Age range
- Identifying Genders (Where applicable)
- Industries (White, pink, blue collar. + Samples of industries)
- Job Titles
- Income (Identify whether they are dual or single income and approximately how much)
- Geographic Location(s)
- For B2B, add:

- Number of Employees
- Annual Revenues
- Number of Business Locations
- Family Life (Married? Single? Divorced? Kids? Pets?)
- Hobbies
- Who do they hang out with?
- Where do they hangout online?
- Where do they hangout offline?
- What memberships do they pay for?
- Where do they get their news?
- Education
- Net Worth
- Number of Cars
- Number of Homes
- *Note: These next items are only filled out if they are positively identifying your ideal buyer segment. I do not recommend or condone using any of these items as a filter to exclude prospects.*
  - Race
  - Sexual Orientation
  - Politics
  - Religion

Psychographics:
- Interests
- Dislikes
- Aspirations
- What information do they need in order to make a buying decision?

Create a folder on your computer or the drive that you keep all your work documents in, and title it "Marketing." Inside, create a sub folder titled "Marketing Plan [Year]". Now either go download the fill-able document from MarketingBeyondSocialMedia.com (Really, it's easier than typing it up yourself and talking yourself into skipping the items that you think aren't relevant – but really are). Then save that document into your Marketing Plan [Year] folder as "Target Market"

Step 1: Fill In The Blanks

Let's start with the easy stuff. Go through the target market and start filling in as many items as you already know. Follow *general* trends. I get that you probably have a pretty broad base of buyers and potential buyers but pull a client list (or ideal persona in your head) and start picking out the trends. Again, remember that your target market shouldn't span more than one generation (usually about 15 years) and should have something that differentiates them from others in that generation. The more specific you can get, the more valuable this will be. Remember that you don't have to limit yourself to just one target market, but each target market should be defined and distinct. Maybe you're targeting single mothers who are millennials with one target market. Another can focus on working professionals in the healthcare industry between 40 and 55 years old.

Whatever information you *do* know, jot it down first. Just fill in as many items as you can. Whatever you put down, you may add more to that section later but what you already know is a great place to start. Because even a well-trained AI chatbot struggles to answer give a good answer to, "Who's my target market?" But it sure can answer, "Where do 30-year-old moms of two hang out offline?" In other words, the more work you do here, the easier the next step will be. Do yourself a favor and set the timer for 15-minutes and force yourself to keep writing until the timer goes off. You'll be impressed at how much info is sleeping in the back corners of your brain that just needs you doing a little spring (or fall or winter!) cleaning to find!

If you're still in pre-revenue mode (i.e. haven't closed your first sale) and do not know *anything* about who is going to buy your product, start looking online to find out information about who is buying similar products or services and log that information. You can adapt and update the data as you start bringing in customers and learning more about who you do and don't want to work with

 Go fill in as many of the blanks on your target market as you can now.

Step 2: Start Researching

The great news is that there are only three steps to building your target market, so you're now 1/3 of the way there!

On the flip side....this research portion will probably take you two to four hours. Minimum. If it takes you less, it's pretty easy to assume you didn't dig deep enough. The goal here is to compile anywhere from six to twelve pages of information on your target market. Unless you *only* want to sell to individuals who have the job title of Director of Sales, do some research to find out the top ten jobs appealing to your ideal gender, age and family-situation. Then ask Google or a well-trained AI chat bot what job titles someone might have in that job. Rinse and repeat for each of the top ten jobs and include all of those under the Job Titles section.

If you know what kinds of job titles your ideal buyer might use, their identified gender and their age range but don't know anything about their family life, use that to frame your google search instead. Try something like, "How many kids do 50-year-old men who work in finance usually have?"

And I know! Some of y'all are crying out already. "Steph! Google is *not* a reliable source and neither are the AI chat bots!"

I get it. Anyone can put anything on the internet. To be fair though, Google has a pretty solid process for ensuring that anything you'll find within the first 10-15 search engine results is solidly backed. But, to ensure all your bases are covered, I recommend using th efollowing perimeters to determine the validity of the info you're finding:

1. If it's been listed in an established database with a good reputation
OR
2. It's published in at least two separate news sources that are recent (within 5 years) and do not reference each other.

This is where using the AI chat bots can be dangerous. They don't always have sources! It can take a minute to get used to scrutinizing your sources like this, but it's a good skill to learn regardless in our growing age of mis and disinformation. Remember, Finding two sources that claim that women in their thirties have five children on average isn't helpful if both sources are from the 1990s, and quoting each other.

As a side note, you can also look to verify information you find online yourself. Imagine you discover that, to your surprise, college students are picking up crocheting and you find that a little suspicious. Go check out some of the crochet groups on places like Reddit, or some of the college student groups. Look at the age of people, or straight up ask a question and see what response you get. Search for hashtags on social platforms and look at who's posting about them. Make sure you're checking the social platforms that your ideal buyer is hanging out on. Checking Facebook for what college students are up to is probably going to be misleading. At least at time of publication for this book.

At this point, I hope it's obvious that Google is your bestie for this process.

But my team and I also leverage databases like Census.gov, Reference USA, and many more. These change regularly as some become 'pay-to-play' or better options crop up, so instead of including a list here that will be out of date eventually, we'll keep a list of the websites that my team and I use for target market research up to date at MarketingBeyondSocialMedia.com!

As another way to verify the information you find online, I highly recommend reaching out to your current clients, or individuals who fit your ideal client details, and requesting permission to ask just a few questions to verify the information. Don't inundate them. Just pick three or four of the categories you're least confident in and ask those. That might look like "My online research says that women like you like to spend their time working out at places like boutique yoga studios, barre classes, etc. Based on you actually *knowing* what you love and don't, do you feel that's accurate?" Or keep it a little wider "What are your favorite places to get a good workout?"

It may sound crazy, but you can even find psychographic information online. Asking "What are women in their mid-thirties with kids most interested in today?" Will reveal a plethora of articles and posts on social platforms. Open a bunch. Read through them. Dig into the groups and comments on blogs, then document the information that is recurring across all of those articles (again, as long as they aren't all referencing each other).

 You guessed it – time to go follow the instructions here and start researching! Fill in the gaps on your Target Market document until you've gotten as far as you possibly can!

Step 3: Educated Guessing

This last step tends to drive people crazy when I mention it. That's the Educated Guessing stage of filling in the Target Market. If you haven't been able to fill in all the gaps, and you don't have anyone you can ask, you'll have to rely on educated guesses. If it makes you feel better, highlight the items you've guessed on as items to verify as soon as you get the chance. But this exercise is extremely helpful to help get into your prospective buyer's head. It's time to ask yourself: "If I were a mid-twenties young woman starting her career in marketing in New York City, what would I be most afraid of? What would I want most out of life? Where would I hang out online?" If you can, try and pretend you're your ideal buyer and walk a day in their shoes (in your mind of course!). You can always then go online and try to verify your guesses as well but I've often found that, if I've done the other research thoroughly, my guesses tend to be pretty on-point.

Fiction writers do a variation of this all the time. When I started working seriously on my fiction pieces, I often sat down and would just write about the characters sitting down for dinner. It would tell me so much about them. How they ate. Where they ate. When they ate. What they ate. How they moved. What they thought about when they ate. Seriously, give it a try sometime! You might learn that your ideal buyer spends her evenings, three nights a week, at a martial arts studio because she is afraid of what might happen on the streets if she's untrained. Or that she settled for a crappy apartment near her work because she doesn't like taking the subway.

This is a great exercise to do once a year, even if you've got your target market nailed down. It's what helps us take a target market and turn it into a persona, and also get creative about how we're going to put our marketing message in front of them in a way they will see and care.

Go back to your Target Market document and fill in the last blanks with your educated guesses.

The Marketing Message

This is one of my favorite parts of marketing. Building the emotionally evocative message. One that will spur the buyer to action. One that is memorable. One that gives the small business plenty to talk about and plenty of ways to market themselves beyond just talking about the day-to-day of what they do. When I have these conversations, I almost always have to start by differentiating between the tagline and the message.

I've seen *many* small business owners spiral into hours upon hours of trying to nail down the perfect, punchy tagline! The one that is going to make them go viral. The one that will perfectly encapsulate what they do that what makes them special. The one that will be memorable enough that everyone will instantly recall them until the end of time – or at least every time they need to buy.

They are starting in the wrong spot.

Remember back in Marketing Craves Creativity when I talked about one of the biggest takeaways you'll ever find for anything, but especially marketing? There are no silver bullets in marketing. The people who put together a funnel that converts tens of thousands or even millions just from a series of landing pages and social media ads, didn't start with that. They built a brand, a network, and refined and honed messaging over a long time. They put out messaging that wasn't great and it just got buried in the stuff that was.

The people who have gone viral with seemingly effortless drops of a video (or tagline or logo, or a video, etc) didn't do it overnight. One of my favorite interviews ever was with a CEO named Jason Straughan. Jason was part of the team that co-founded a major tech school headquartered in San Antonio called

Code-Up and he participated in a series I released online long ago called "How You Got Here." In our interview, Jason shared his whole story of starting his first business, a computer repair store in a mall. That business didn't last long. Neither did the next. In fact, he had a string of what were definitely failures by every external measurement. Then, in what seemed sudden to everyone on the outside, he found huge success with Code-Up. He laughed when he got to this part of the interview and said, "I guess I'm just a 40-year overnight success story."

That staggered me. But the more I looked around, the more I saw it everywhere. Authors who suddenly burst onto the scene and were everywhere with one major book. But when I looked closer, they always had a series of tries behind that book. Michael Dubin and the Dollar Shave Club story were one of my favorites to self-flagellate over for years. If Dubin could build a business that was worth billions in under four years, I should be able to do it in five, right?

But the truth is, for all of us and in every area from business to marketing, we're all multi-year overnight success stories. The likelihood that one thing is going to go viral right off the bat is slim. So stop stressing about finding the perfect tagline. Your message is *much* bigger than your tagline anyhow. A great tagline will spark from a solid marketing message. Not the other way around.

So what is the marketing message?

I'm glad you asked! The marketing message is the overarching story that you're working to communicate to your target market. This document is also probably *not* going to be public facing. But it will drive everything that is. It will drive the decisions you make about the colors you use, the quality of material creation you invest in, and so much more.

The first time I caught a real glimpse of this concept in action was in 2017. Years prior, I'd picked up a book by one of my favorite marketing authors, Seth Godin, called *All Marketers Are Liars Tell Stories*. In 2017, I finally got around to reading it (Thanks ADHD). It blew my mind. He told a story that struck me about how a veggie chip company arranged to have their chips placed in the veggie section of the grocery store during their launch. They understood that their target market was exhausted mothers who wanted to do good for their kids. Having the chips readily available, in a matte-bag covered in natural greens and oranges and yellows, in the veggie section, said to the mothers "This is an easy, healthy middle-ground for your kids!" Better than that, it gave these moms the ability to live up to their mental image of being a good mom, while also grabbing something their kids would eat.

It was the first time I started to understand that messaging is more than *what* you say. Messaging is the way you choose to communicate that message. It's how you say it. If I try and tell you that my job is to make your life easier, but it's complicated to book a consult, hire me, find (or even navigate) my website, I'm not really making your life easier, am I? And, as the cliches go, "a picture is worth a thousand words" and "talk is cheap."

I can say that I want to make you feel better about yourself all I want, but if my marketing is making you feel inadequate and unable to live up, are you going to believe that attending my event is going to make you feel better?

Absolutely not.

Messaging should drive how your business represents itself to the marketplace.

For example, Grow Disrupt offers an event coined The Growcation. It's branded as a luxury working vacation with intimate access to a celebrated expert. Attendance is extremely limited. In turn, we are tremendously careful about how we market it. We take our cues from the luxury vehicle industry. The marketing is less in-your-face and every single piece of marketing that hits the market is impeccably designed. This is the instance when I'll spring for the expensive, linen-style cardstock or the high-quality matte finish to the print-out. All our logos are designed by actual graphic designers, but this one in particular has to draw in simplicity and elegance. It has to feel luxurious from the first glance.

Instead of sending out a generic postcard to interested guests, I personally compose a custom box. In 2021 our guest was Jesse Cole, the owner of the Savannah Bananas. I spent a few hours experimenting in the kitchen to perfect a toasted oat, cinnamon and rum banana bread recipe. Then I made minis of those banana breads and sent them in a small box along with a banana-shaped stress toy and a personalized letter to each person inviting them to the event. Was it a lot of extra work? Yup! Was it worth it? Yup! Because I can't promise that this is an event 'built around you' and then send out generic promotional material about it. If I do, I've got a promise that is not being represented in my marketing!

The result? Almost 30% of the people who received them posted about the event on their social media and it was the impetus to close three additional sales for the event. That was roughly four hours of work plus $125 in supplies and shipping for roughly $20,000 in revenue. I'll make that trade every single day.

And in pursuit of sharing the things that hasn't worked, I can't tell you the number of postcards we printed and shipped to potential guests for The Grow Retreat between 2018 and 2020. That was probably a few thousand dollars, and never once have we generated a sale from those postcards. Even when we tried customizing them to the individual recipient.

On another note of things that didn't work, I had a client once who wanted their message to revolve around how "we make your life easier by [insert their primary function]." But their website was legitimately so complicated to navigate, had so many pages that led nowhere, and even their contact page wasn't super helpful (A form to fill out, nothing more). Thousands of visitors to the website monthly weren't even converting to their newsletter.

To sum up: whatever your message is, your presentation needs to back it. If you promise luxury to your prospective clients through what you say, you need to back it up with every aspect of your marketing exuding luxury from design to material. If you promise uniqueness to your client, you need to back it up by only doing marketing that stands out and has some element of uniqueness to it. At the very least, tear the edges of the fliers so that each one truly is unique. If you promise ease, you guessed it, you need to make it easy to find and convert to working with you.

As an added perk, once we've figured out what the marketing message is and have a detailed target market, coming up with creative ways to share marketing that stands out to that audience becomes markedly easier. For example, most postcards are recyclable, right? But what if you choose one that was matte and soft, and added a Recycle sign with the phrase "Don't forget to toss me in the recycle bin when you're done! It's easy…just like our program!" That goes a long way towards backing the message that we make recycling easy! Or what if you offer to make getting a healthy dinner easy? That really backs the idea that we not only understand you, but we also are truly part of your team. If I promise that I *get* ADHD individuals and can build an entire event around them, but my website is a block of text or easy to get distracted on, I'm not reinforcing that. If I tell people that our events are an experience unlike anything they've had before, but our marketing looks like other events, or it never gives them a real experience *just* through the marketing, I *will* miss out. One of the most important things we learned to do was to *stop* doing free events. There was just no way we could truly recreate the experience of our events for free. Instead, we focused on getting better at showing the individual elements of our events through great videos. We wrote, produced and released an entire pop ballad and official music video that is an anthem to what it means to be an entrepreneur. A pop ballad that sparks emotion just by listening to the lyrics.

Let's get practical. In practical terms, what is the marketing message?

It's a paragraph that basically tells a story about your ideal buyer, why they're awesome, what they're struggling with in regard to your industry, and how you help them beyond your functional skill. The great news? I've got a fill-in-the-blank template that will serve to start you off. Though your messaging will probably grow and evolve a few times over and it will be up to you to wordsmith it down into something smooth and catchy.

Let's walk through a couple steps that are important to make filling in that template easy.

How to Identify Your Marketing Message: The Mission

It's quite difficult to uncover your unique, emotionally evocative marketing message if you don't know your company mission statement. Your mission statement should be unique to you as well, and it is the spark that your messaging will grow out of, so let's start there.

Even if you think you already know your mission statement, skim this next section just to be sure we're on the same page. I've learned over the years that there are a lot of different perspectives on what a mission statement is but since this is integral to how I have found the best messaging, it's important we're eye-to-eye here.

I understand that everyone has a different concept of what differentiates a vision and a mission. I've seen some credible individuals argue that the vision is a single sentence goal for the company to accomplish. But the lines start getting blurry on the difference between that and the mission. To me, they often sound identical. I'm assuming I'm not the only person who's ended up absolutely lost here.

Whenever there is some confusion about what a word means, as mentioned before, I tend to go back to the root of those words. The root of "Vision" is the Latin verb "Vis" which means "To See." To me, that means that the vision is about what you see for the future of the company. It's the blueprint of what you're building. The tangible aspects of what the future of the company looks like. A good vision is typically a paragraph or so about what you're building. It should mention who you're selling to (in a single sentence). It is also what you'll provide, how you'll deliver it, and what your brand will represent. It's probably not an external document, but it should serve to give you and your team a clear idea of what they are building! It's a description of what you'll see when you get to the top of Mt. Everest!

As a side note, I find that this is indispensable for culture building. The day-to-day of running and working in a small business can be mundane. As the business owner, I am usually pretty good at keeping my eye on the long-term goal. But my team is not. It's not *their* vision, so I don't blame them. Having the vision in writing where they can see it, and where I can reference back and review it with them once a quarter in our team meetings? It's priceless. I always see their eyes light up when we go over the vision of what we're building. I notice energy and motivation from them that wasn't there before. This document is helpful for more than just having an eye on the future.

The mission statement is different. This is a single sentence that encompasses what need your business fills and why it's allowed to continue existing.

Let me explain.

I remember in high school learning about the floor and ceiling in economics and being intrigued. The idea that if a business can't stay relevant or keep its price inside of what the market will bear, it will find itself shut down just blew my mind. I've learned a bit since then, and obviously there are always anomalies, but some principles stand. For example, if your business isn't filling a need at a price point people are willing to pay for that solution, it won't get to stick around. And if your business is filling the same need as a million others, someone is going to find a way to do it cheaper. That means you're going to be functioning close to commodity level, which means you'll be fighting the price-sensitive situation constantly. That is an exhausting battle to run and one I don't think most small businesses are poised to win.

Your mission statement should be what you provide to the marketplace that is both unique and needed. This way you get to command the price point for your product or service that works for you to thrive in business.

Side note, if you're fighting pricing battles constantly and losing clients over prices that are just a few pennies apart, you're a commodity and your business is in danger. Your job is to find a way to elevate and stand out. It's not easy, but it's doable in nearly every industry. You and your business deserve it. So take this next section very seriously because this is going to be the difference maker for you.

If you're being told that you're too expensive but then people are spending more money elsewhere, you're not a commodity, your marketing just doesn't match up to the price you're asking.

Let's think about what a mission is real quick.

Picture a spy, sitting on a bench in a park, casually reading a newspaper. Their contact arrives and sits next to them, feigning casual meeting as he delivers the code word. The spy returns the counter-code. Still as casual as you can be, the contact rises to leave and neglects to grasp his briefcase. Not long later, the spy rises and leaves as well with the briefcase in hand. Back in some crummy, dark apartment, our spy enters the code to open the briefcase. Inside is a sheet of paper with a single sentence on it. The spy's next mission. For the next 48-hours, this spy will exist solely to fulfill that mission. They will focus on "Extracting the flash drive from the vault at the embassy" or "Assassinate the king of Exelmoldovia." Ok, hopefully not the latter (Especially because that's clearly not a real country). But everything they do from that moment on will be focused on how to accomplish that mission.

I believe our mission statement for our businesses should be the same thing. A single sentence goal that explains why we exist. Some of the mission statements I've helped come up with for my companies, myself, and my clients are:

"To be the golden standard in the water treatment industry."

"To support small business owner growth through maximizing profits."

"To create a world where others recognize the power of personal choice."

"To empower ADHD small business owners to thrive personally and professionally."

One of my favorite authors, Mike Michalowicz, embraces "To eradicate entrepreneurial poverty."[7]

You might notice a couple of trends. These all fit on one line and they all start with the infinitive form of a verb. An infinitive (the stem of a verb preceded by "to") shows a state of being. This is who we are. It should evoke emotion in you. It should be the simplest form of a sentence that you could elaborate on for hours with little to no notice. And it should be unique to *you*. If you could apply this mission statement to anyone else in your industry, it's too generic and you're risking falling into the world of commodity.

For example, Grow Disrupt's mission statement is to empower ADHD small business owners to thrive personally and professionally. I get fired up when I start thinking about this. It started for me years ago back when my coaching practice was the primary bread-winner for the business. I was sitting at a little Vietnamese café opposite a client and he was telling me about the previous night. He'd been playing with his kids on the carpet and had to call a halt to the play because he couldn't breathe. He found himself laying on the carpet, holding his chest, staring up at the ceiling and wondering if he was having a heart attack. He

_____

7 Fair note, I did not help him come up with this. He's just brilliant all on his own!

was the same age as me and in impeccable physical condition. He was running a multi-million-dollar company that was fielding buy-offers regularly, and he was just about broken. His business was thriving. He was not.

I was struck. It was the first time I really started to see the cycle that I'd heard about so many times. So many small business owners end up putting all of their energy and life into building a successful business. Only to have to step away to put their personal life in order. Their health falls apart or their spouse decides they are done and files for divorce. Once the intrepid entrepreneur has picked up the pieces there to some semblance of repair, they dive back into the business to get it back on track. And a little later, they'll step away again to get their personal life put back together. And again. And again. And again. A year prior to that moment in the cafe, a gentleman I'd looked up to immensely had to step away from building his business because his wife surprised him with divorce papers. It's not an uncommon situation. And it's heartbreaking.

Small business owners put their heart and soul into building a business that takes care of their employees and provides a better service or product than the vast majority of their competitors. The small business owner is the first person to the office (and the last to leave). They pick up the slack when things go wrong. They wear too many hats. They're dealing with the most upset customers. They're working weekends. And they're working on vacation. They are usually the first ones to take pay cuts when things get tight.

And I understand this isn't *always* the case. *But it is more often than not.* And for them to put in that much work, that much heart and passion, and to end up taking pay cut after pay cut when things get tight breaks my heart. For their personal lives to fall apart while they are trying so hard to help others put their lives together, is simply wrong.

Ok! See what I mean? Get me going and I could write a book about this. Your mission statement should spark the same kind of passion in you.

So how do you find your mission statement if you don't know it already?

When I'm working with someone to find their mission statement, we start with identifying the answer to the question: "Why do people buy from you? No… why do they *really* buy from you?"

No one is buying an event ticket. No one is buying a marketing course. People are buying someone who understands how their brain operates and not just provides the content, but also support on getting that idea implemented in their business. That's a much better answer. Ultimately, it's still not the reason people are buying from me and Grow Disrupt, but it's a good start. Once I know that 'pretty good' reason, I can follow the Rule of Five Whys. The Rule of Five Whys is based on the idea that when you ask an initial question, you get the initial and obvious answer. If you ask Why that answer exists, and then why *that* answer exists, five times over, you'll find the root of the situation. In engineering, this gives us the opportunity to solve the root of the problem instead of slapping a band-aid on that will stop working in a few months. In finding your mission statement, we're going to follow a similar process.

But this is more than just about your buyer. This is *your* mission statement.

Our goal is to ask Why until we feel we've reached the *real* reason the buyer comes to you. Then we're going to switch that up and ask ourselves: "Why does this matter to me?" In my experience, we'll ask Why more than just five times, but if you aim for at least five, you know you'll get pretty close!

For example! Since I've already talked about where my fire for Grow Disrupt comes from, let's look at *why* I'm talking about marketing and started building a personal brand in 2021 just to do so on a wider scale.

1st Why: Why do people buy marketing help from me? (Whether that's a book, a Spark Lab, a Done-For-You Marketing Plan, etc).

1st Answer: There are a lot of reasons but primarily because they want to organize their marketing strategy and get more effective marketing without breaking the bank.

2nd Why: Great! Why do they care about that?

2nd Answer: Because they are passionate about building their business and they know more revenue is key and marketing makes that revenue a *lot* easier to generate.

3rd Why: Great! Why do they care about that?

3rd Answer: Maybe they know in their gut that their product or service is *direly* needed on the marketplace, and they want to change their industry. Maybe they want to replace their full-time income like I did in 2014 and walk away to be a full-time entrepreneur. Maybe they *need* to increase their income to take care of their family. Either way, they've got some goal they are passionate about and building their business will empower that. And they are tired of not getting the results they know they should be getting. They are tired of getting overlooked. They're tired of being the bridesmaid and never the bride in the sales conversation.

That answer feels emotionally charged and is probably pretty close to exactly why people choose to buy from me when it comes to marketing. Once I've found a strongly emotional answer to the first question, I will switch gears to ask myself "So why does this matter to me?"

4th Why: Why do *I* care about that?

4th Answer: Because I was in those shoes and trying to figure out the same thing in 2016, 2017 and 2018 for our events. It was heartbreakingly frustrating to struggle for others to see what I was so excited about in a way that spurred them to take action and buy a ticket. I knew that our method of putting on events was desperately needed. The event industry was, to say the least, a mess. Event producers have been more interested in turning a profit for years than in providing actual content and value for their attendees. They cram people into a room, shoulder-to-shoulder, fill the room with too-loud music, too few breaks, and too much content. The stage is filled with pitch after pitch. There are usually one or two flagship speakers that everyone is excited to hear from that *may* provide real content. The rest of the speakers provide little to no real value and pitch on pie-in-the-sky promises. The set-up works because attendees are then so physically, emotionally, and mentally exhausted that they have little resistance to the pitch. On the off chance that the guests recover enough from the event to realize they don't want what they purchased within the cancellation window, attempts to cancel the purchase after the event are usually met with gaslighting and shame. It's a mess.

Despite knowing all that, I struggled to communicate what we were doing to others. Worse, I spent a lot of money to hire some coaches who gave me woefully inadequate information on how to communicate it better. I look back and realize that those coaches put me in dangerous positions. Not just financially after dropping $6,000 I didn't have to spare on a "marketing course" that turned out to be nine-hours of recorded group coaching sessions to muddle through and figure out how to apply to my business. But also emotionally and energetically. I was exhausted after fighting with them over how we did events and what mattered to me to show in our marketing. They didn't *get* what I was doing. They wanted me to re-structure our events to match the industry average so we could use industry standards for marketing. And they tried to have me use the exact same branding and marketing as every other self-help event. Based on everything you've read so far, I'm sure you can see where the problem with that advice was.

It was the wasted energy that was the worst. As we've established a few times, energy is the most precious resource. When I see someone else in the same situation I was in, what worries me most is knowing that they are getting closer and closer to giving up, and their brilliance may never truly be seen. There are hundreds of people like me out there who are getting *this* close to never getting to shine. That breaks my heart.

5th Why: Why does *that* matter to me?

5th Answer: Because the people who are attracted to work with me are working on something *incredible*. These people deserve to succeed. They want to build a business that will take care of others and change industries. They do not deserve to be taken advantage of by someone who succeeded a couple of times in marketing but doesn't know the actual process behind it and especially doesn't understand the nuance of small business marketing. More importantly, they need ongoing support. I hate courses that are limited time-access or come with only limited ongoing support. First because I'm ADHD and I will 100% forget to finish the course before access expires. And two, because I'm ADHD and I need some ongoing support on figuring out how to apply it to my business sometimes.

And I know I'm not alone. I want to help others like me.

(Stephanie here with a quick aside from the exercise, at this point, I feel like this answer is pretty good…but it's also pretty lengthy. So I have two options, ask Why again, or try and distill this down into a single, short sentence. I'll usually try the second option first and see if I can get it distilled down. If I can't, I usually haven't found the core *of the mission.)*

The distilled version 1: I believe that people who are working on something incredible to change lives deserve success. Not be beaten down by poorly crafted programs that are designed to support the marketer selling the course more than the entrepreneur buying it. A lot of times that comes down to getting access to *good* education that works for how their ADHD responds!

(Steph again - this is close! Let's see if we can take it down a little further and get it to a single sentence.)

Distillation #2: I'm passionate about supporting ADHD industry changers like myself in getting their message heard.

To put this into the formula for our mission statement: To support other ADHD industry disrupters in ensuring their message is heard!

There you go! A single, short sentence that gets me *fired* up! Once again, we've discovered a sentence that I could talk about for hours before I run out of things to say. One could argue that I've lost sight of the nuance of the emotion by distilling it down. But the act of going through the exercise embeds this information in me. Just seeing that one sentence will flood me with a rush of memories from this exercise. My goal is to distill things down to keep them short and sweet so I can keep them front of mind. I'm not going to read a whole paragraph regularly. I *will* glance up from my desk to see the mission statement on the wall, recognize the shape of it, and let it spur me to action. And even though I don't always publicly list my mission statements on our websites, when I do share it with someone, I have something to talk about!

How to Identify Your Marketing Message: The Message

Great news! We've got a beautiful foundation to build our marketing message on now. And by its nature of tapping into something that *you* are unbelievably passionate about, it's going to be different than your competition. Not only that, but this is going to gear you up to be able to communicate that marketing message a hundred different ways. Have you ever looked at someone who never seems to run out of things to say about their business? That is a person who understands their marketing message! One of my favorite examples of this is Ami Feller with The Roofer Chicks. Ami has established an incredible brand with her pink-caped superhero, Lucy, who flies in to save the day and fix your roof. Ami is one of only a few companies in the entire country to have an all-women roofing crew, goes above and beyond to empower women in the trades, and be an active part of her community.

But as much of their brand is built to empower women in the trades, Ami's message actually comes down to: "We're here to take care of our community." In a practical sense, they do that by taking care of the roofs of their community. But Ami lives and breathes this message. She is plugged into her community of New Braunfels, TX in a hundred different ways. She cheers on her fellow small business owners online and off. She participates in an incredible number of give-back initiatives personally and with her whole company. I don't think a week goes by that she's not plugged in doing something incredible for the people around her. And you can see it in their marketing online, how they were chosen to be featured on Good Morning America in 2023, and the countless awards and accolades that come their way every year.

There are two primary lines of thought on how to build a marketing message in the marketing community. The first being that your messaging needs to show your prospective buyer how they are inadequate without you. This kind of messaging is built to spark fear emotions, shame, and open a 'light at the end of the tunnel' offer that only comes when the prospect buys from that provider. If you've seen marketing that made you feel inadequate or a little anxious, you've probably seen marketing that appeals to this line of thinking. If you've been involved with a provider that made you feel incompetent without them or that they are the only path forward, you've been exposed to this line of marketing.

The second is to uplift your buyer and help them feel better about themselves before they even purchase. This line of thinking focuses on ensuring your prospect sees how great they are and understanding that they are going to be a better version of themselves with you. I personally prefer the second type of marketing for two reasons:

I don't like putting other people down or making them doubt or question themselves to get them to work with me...that feels manipulative and slimy.

This type of marketing tends to attract psychologically healthier individuals. And those people are more fun to work with.

Not only would I rather work with a healthy individual who wants support over a savior, but we tend to get better results too. First, personally, I'm not here to save anyone. It took me years to realize that. Once I did, it was a huge weight off my shoulders. All I want to do is support people who are trying to make the world a better place. Secondly, those are the people who take what I give them and apply it and extrapolate it and produce exponential results!

Because of this, every marketing message I create, and support others in creating, is going to align with the second messaging theory. If you're looking for the first option, I'm not the right person to learn from. I won't teach it. I don't condone it.

The best part? This next step is like building a house! You took the time to get to know your target market and build your mission statement. That's like creating the initial plans and letting the foundation cure. It takes a while, but this next part is about to bring it all together. You ready?

Write down one or two sentences about how *amazing* your ideal buyer is! Examples:

The Impact Authority: "The people who turn to us for help are passionate visionaries looking to make the world a better place. These individuals are superpowered by their ADHD perspective on the world and are constantly searching to better enable that superpower!"

Grow Disrupt: "Our event guests are passionate visionaries who are changing the world through ripple effects and business practices that disrupt traditional commercial humbug. They put their people first and care deeply about their teams, their clients, and sometimes themselves too."

Notice how this is purely about *them*? This is not talking about why they buy from me. Or why they are so easy to sell to. Or who they are in relation to my service at all. This is purely about what is cool about *them*.

Write About how Amazing Your Ideal Buyer Is Here:

(Remember, this needs to focus on how they are incredible! What you love about working with them! Not why they buy from you. What makes them unique?)

Got yours? Great! Next, write down the challenge that they have as it relates to your industry, i.e.: the problem that you help them solve.
Examples:
The Impact Authority: "Our clients sometimes find themselves overwhelmed with their marketing and need help organizing it to ensure consistent delivery, and/or are frustrated that their output isn't making the impact they want in their marketplace."
Grow Disrupt: "They are also frequently caught up in the minutiae of running a business and lose sight of themselves and their vision – and they hate going to events that just make them feel overwhelmed and worse about themselves, despite knowing it's important."

Write Down the Challenge Your Buyer Has With Your Industry:

On point! Let's move to the last part. The last sentence we're going to add here is what we provide that helps. Once again, keep it short and sweet.

Examples:

The Impact Authority: "We provide marketing structure and ongoing creative support and accountability for these visionaries so they can execute, make an impact, and light a marketing engine that can't be stopped."

Grow Disrupt: "We create space for these visionaries to reconnect and rediscover themselves and their own capabilities while empowering business growth by providing practical tools and application at our events."

Write How You Help Here:

Fan-freaking-tastic! Let's put it all together:

The Impact Authority: "The people who turn to us for help are passionate visionaries looking to make the world a better place. These individuals are superpowered by their ADHD perspective, and are constantly searching to better enable that superpower! Our clients sometimes find themselves overwhelmed with their marketing and need help organizing it to ensure consistent delivery, and/or are frustrated that their output isn't making the impact they want in their marketplace. We provide marketing structure and ongoing creative support and accountability for these visionaries so they can execute, make an impact, and light a marketing engine that can't be stopped."

Grow Disrupt: "Our guests are passionate visionaries that are changing the world through ripple effects and business practices that disrupt traditional commercial humbug. They put their people first and care deeply about their teams, their clients, and sometimes themselves too. They are also frequently caught up in the minutiae of running a business and lose sight of themselves and their vision – and they hate going to events that just make them feel overwhelmed and worse about themselves, despite knowing it's important. We create space for them to reconnect and rediscover themselves and their own capabilities while empowering business growth by providing practical tools and application at our events."

It's pretty cool right! To see exactly what you're doing and why distilled down into a short paragraph that you can use to spark all *kinds* of creative marketing messages to put out there.[8]

Now you can wordsmith that down a few times over until you've got it down to something relatively short, specific, and easy to remember:

The Impact Authority: "Our clients are passionate visionaries who make the world a better place and deserve marketing systems and support that doesn't overwhelm and frustrate them so they can make the impact they deserve."

Grow Disrupt: "Our guests are passionate visionaries. We create space for them to keep an eye on how incredible they are and empower their business growth by providing practical tools and application at our events."

---

8 Don't panic if you're not already brimming with ideas, we'll talk more about this in a minute and I've got lots of inspiration for you!

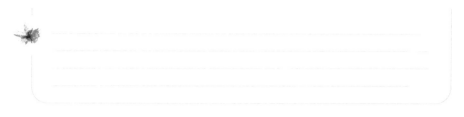

It may take a while to get to where you can wordsmith down your message as concise as I have. That's okay. It took me a while too! Do your best but relax. As long as you've got the longer paragraph, the next part is easy enough!

The next part of the marketing messaging is to understand how to Show-Don't-Tell your message and this is where it starts getting really fun…so let's go!

Before you move on however, make sure you've got this beautiful creation saved in a file in that Marketing folder that you set up earlier! I like to title my document "Marketing Message [Year]."

How to Show-Don't-Tell, Your Marketing Message

The Kay Jewelers Example:

When I present this training from the front of the room, I almost always use Kay Jewelers as an example here. Because, for a long time, their marketing messaging was on-point and so beautifully shown. While their tagline has been "Every Kiss Begins with Kay," that's not really the message they are communicating. Because, frankly, no one is buying a diamond in exchange for a kiss. That would be silly. When I ask my listeners who is going to buy a diamond in exchange for a kiss, I get chuckles and shakes of heads. We all know it's a bit of a weird industry to try and market. But Kay has done it and been a leader in the industry for years.

Because they are not selling a kiss. They are selling you a moment that brings you closer to the person you love. And for a long time, they showcased that in every commercial. Every single commercial showed two people further apart in the beginning who came closer together by the end. A gal waiting at a restaurant, obviously for a date, the guy coming to the restaurant to meet his girlfriend for dinner. He proposes, they hug and kiss. End commercial.

The next one might show a mom comforting a kid in the nursery, and the dad waking up and seeing them on the baby monitor. Dad gets up and comes into the nursery to surprise mom with a diamond necklace for Mother's Day. They literally start in different rooms, then come closer together and hug at the end.

One of my favorites is a commercial that stars CGI penguins. In the commercial, a male penguin approaches a female and nudges a rock towards her while the narrator advises that some penguins will show love by offering a pebble. The female penguin considers the pebble, then turns away and snubs him. The narrator then adds that, "Some penguins are a little smarter." The next shot shows a penguin nudging a Kay Jewelers box with a diamond pendant towards the female penguin. The young lady penguin glances at it, then the next shot is the two snuggling. Literally coming closer together once again.

These old ads are a brilliant and consistent example of how to Show-Don't-Tell your marketing. Because we'll definitely spend thousands of dollars to create a moment where we'll be drawn closer to the person we care about.

But Kay Jewelers isn't the only one who does this. I've littered this entire book with examples of how to Show-Don't-Tell your message. The textile recycling business who made it easy (and green) to get involved, reinforcing his message that recycling can be easy and green. The medical practice billing consultant who gave doctors free, healthy meals to show them that she understood them and was on their side. My handcrafted boxes of a next-level banana bread and individual note to showcase how special, personalized and next-level the Growcation is. I also make a point to, frequently, post simple, basic videos talking about how easy marketing can be. Easy videos that I piece together in under a few minutes. Because I want the message to be backed up by the actual method of distribution. If I'm going to say marketing is easy, it's not going to reinforce that message if I've got explosions and animation going on in the background or rely purely on production quality videos.

But I also recognize that this is...kind of hard! So I'm going to take a few pages here to give a few more examples of how to do this. If you've already got some great ideas on how to do this and don't need some "inspo pages," you can skip to the next bolded header. If you do...keep reading!

I'm also going to leave space at the bottom of each story, with a prompt, for you to write your own ideas based on the sample just provided!

Prompt: In the Kay Jewelers example, we get to see how you can physically show something in a video commercial. How can

you physically show your marketing message in video form? Jot
down a few ideas below. Remember, no idea is a bad idea and you
can worry about execution later:

The Grow Retreat Example

Jesse Cole, the owner of the Savannah Bananas, once said to me, "If you aren't your biggest fan, how can you expect anyone else to be?" And it stuck with me! So pardon me a minute if I rave about some of the things we have done, I'm a big fan!

The Grow Retreat is the flagship event for Grow Disrupt but when I hosted the first Grow Retreat in 2017, I had no real idea how to market an event. To be fair, I had only some basic ideas of how to put on the kind of event that The Grow Retreat has grown into! But I knew, at its heart, it was different from other events. Even from the beginning, we didn't allow pitching from our speakers. We required our speakers to sit onsite, throughout the event, at the same tables as the guests. Those were two of our biggest differences at first. In year two, we expanded to two days and added some pretty incredible swag bags. By year three, we'd found our formula of Day 1 being dedicated to Ideation and Day 2 being all about Application. We also started bringing in some serious heavy hitters for speakers, like Mike Michalowicz, and still convinced them to hang out onsite and be accessible to our guests. That was the first year we added a theme for our content to revolve around as well.

Leading up to the 2020 retreat, we landed on the tagline "Unlike anything you've experienced before." But as I've alluded to before, our marketing and branding was pretty identical to every other educational event out there. Golds and greens in the branding. A landing page. Some social media posts and ads. Emails to my list. And that was about it. It didn't really do much for reinforcing that marketing message.

Leading up to the 2020 retreat, I commissioned a custom brand to be built for the event to revolve around the theme. At the time, I thought we'd keep the same brand for the event year after year. I realized quickly that commissioning a new brand annually was a phenomenal way to help reinforce the message. If the brand changed annually, it literally showed the messaging through that continued evolution.

I also quickly realized that keeping our themes to short words helped reinforce that this event is built for those with short attention spans (ADHD entrepreneurs). So while our first theme was Eukairia (Not just long, but also hard to spell and understand!) and our second was Immersion, our third was Impact, then Connect, Shift, and Spark successively. Not only that, but ensuring every brand featured bright, vibrant colors meant it would stand out and spark energy, just like the event itself. The brand quickly became a powerful way for us to show, not just tell, our messaging.

Then I had to clean up the landing pages. We built out a full website for the event. And got professional designers to go in and elevate the graphic elements and flow of the site. If this was going to be the online home of The Grow Retreat, I wanted it to be as enjoyable to navigate as the event itself. I've spent years refining and refining that website. Listening to the questions people asked, then ensuring that information is easy to find on the site.

Next up, I started to focus on how to give others the chance to experience a taste of what it is like at the retreat through our marketing. As mentioned before, for years I experimented with free micro events. I ran structured masterminds quarterly. We had an application process in place so everyone had to pass some level of qualifying to get into the room, just like the actual Grow Retreat. I worked hard to line up some exclusive venues. We put out great food and drinks. But ultimately, free is free. I didn't have the latitude to really make it match The Grow Retreat experience. There is an element of wonder when a Grow Retreat guest walks into a room that we've spent fourteen months designing top to bottom that cannot be replicated for a free event. Especially when we usually had half-an-hour or less of access to set up. Eventually, as much as I loved them, I had to retire the Think and Grow Masterminds for the good of our marketing.

Instead, we added a micro event called the ReConnects. These micro events are included with registration to the upcoming Grow Retreat and attendance is only available to registered guests. Basically, unless you're registered for The Grow Retreat, you can't go to a ReConnect. If you are registered, the ReConnect is one of the best freebies on the list of things we do for our guests! The goal of the ReConnects are not to provide education per se but rather to create space in the busy calendar of the small business owner to come hang out with other business owners in a space where they can relax, share, and just connect. We also knew that if we wanted to do this, we were going to have to ensure that there was some kind of draw to get them out of their office and onsite for the micro event. These are business owners who have a million things on their plate, and they tend to put themselves last. So taking time out of their day to go hang out with other business owners? It's rarely a priority. The good news is, because it's part of the grow Retreat, I could rationalize giving myself a budget to work with.

Knowing that free events just don't have enough of a draw for these guests, even with the exclusivity factor of only being available to registered guests, we had to amp it up. It had to be bucket-list worthy (or at least intriguing enough to get them out of the office!). In 2021 we got reservations at a pre fixe experiential dining restaurant that sells out months in advance for a nine-course dinner. In 2022 we started by taking them up for a sunrise hot air balloon ride. The next quarter we chartered a yacht and took them out for a sunset yacht party. In the last quarter of the year, we took them to an internationally renowned brunch on the gulf. Most importantly, for the purposes of this book, we *very* carefully documented each ReConnect. Those videos and pictures got turned into emotionally evocative videos that we shared online. And it makes more of an impact to see the actual people you *want* to hang out with laughing on a yacht, or with massive grins as they float over the Texas Hill Country. It sparks a little FOMO (fear of missing out) but also, when it's done right, it also creates a spark of joy to watch and listen to that video. It's an echo of what they'll experience onsite. But it's an echo that gives them a hint of what's waiting on the other side.

Speaking of videos, that became a priority for us quickly. Videos can translate a whole slew of emotions in 60-seconds and tend to get a lot more actual absorption versus a lengthy email. So I started pushing the team to work on our video editing skills. Our first few were lacking to say the least. But we kept pushing and we got a *lot* better at creating videos that bring together the excitement, energy, and passion of the retreat into promotional videos for the event itself. Our promotional videos now really capture a glimpse of what it's like at the events themselves. I encourage you to look up Grow Disrupt on YouTube and see some of them for yourself.

My team has learned how to create a video that is on-point when it comes to building anticipation, threading motivation, and increasing excitement in the viewer. As a final aside regarding videos, any video under 60-seconds (and most of our videos are!) are focused on showcasing only one aspect of the event at a time. For example, I did one video just showcasing that we crafted two custom tea blends just for the 2023 retreat. A separate video then showed how one of the blends literally shifted colors (our theme was Shift) when you add lemon juice. If I'd tried to do them both as one, it would have been overwhelming for the viewers and I'd have gotten a *lot* fewer views. Most importantly, I would have actually failed to reinforce the message that this is built for ADHD entrepreneurs because I would have tried to cram too much info into one aspect. That's not ADHD friendly.

One of my favorite Show-Don't-Tell marketing initiatives for the Grow Retreat was the release of the official music video for Fly – An Entrepreneur's Journey on October 6th, 2023. We began the process of writing and composing the entrepreneurial anthem in May of that year. The goal, originally, was to just have a modern-feeling song I could use for my keynote for the upcoming retreat. When Susannah finished putting together the lyrics I came up with into an actual song and came back to me with the demo however, I knew we had to pursue getting this professionally produced. At some point in that journey, the idea crossed our minds to film and produce an official music video as well. I wouldn't necessarily call this entire project one of my lowest cost marketing initiatives in terms of time, energy *or* money, but it was definitely the most unique. Listeners to the song can actually experience the array of emotions present at the Grow Retreat. It's a quintessential example of Show-Don't-Tell.

Understanding how to better market The Grow Retreat has been, as you can see here, a multi-year process. We've gotten a little better and a little better every year. We've added and mastered one aspect at a time. Just like I try to remember to do when I'm working on the violin. That's critically important to recognize. Once again, I think it can be overwhelming to sit on the other side of a book that is trying to simplify concepts to make them approachable and easy-to-understand. Because we're sitting there reading the final outcome of years of testing and skill-building. But none of us got to where we are overnight. Think of something you're super skilled in and how long it took you to get there. Marketing is the same way and marketing each aspect of your business is no different. Cut yourself some slack, take a deep breath, and jot down a few ideas from The Grow Retreat marketing here that you can apply to marketing *your* business.

The Mint Mobile Example:

It's not much of a secret to my network that I'm a big Ryan Reynolds fan. Not necessarily for that scruff, sparkling eyes, or incredible sense of humor (though obviously they don't hurt), but for his marketing genius. He manages both a personal brand and multiple business brands (Aviation Gin, Mint Mobile, Wrexham AFC) with effortless ease. The man has a pulse on the finger of what's going on culturally and it frequently lands his name in the tabloids in a positive way. He and his media company, Maximum Effort Productions, consistently put out incredible marketing that makes an impact, without necessarily boasting high production value.

While we could talk about how masterfully he manipulates and influences the media regarding the Deadpool franchise, I want to focus specifically on how he manages the Mint Mobile ads. Occasionally these ads show up on TV, but often they are simply released online through social and video hosting platforms. I encourage you to take a minute and look a few up if you can't think of any off the top of your head. There is an inherent, low effort feel to them. They are simple scripts. Simple camera angles. Whenever Ryan is on camera, while he brings that A-list Hollywood charm and characteristic dead-pan humor, he's also always dressed down and casual. Very few ads have him standing on anything other than a green screen. In fact, the low-cost design is something he regularly calls out on the ads themselves. One ad in particular jokes about a new director which, as the ad goes on, becomes apparent is intended to be one of his kids. It's a perfect example of Show-Don't-Tell when their messaging is all about how cheap and un-complicated they are in comparison to their competitors.

None of us are stupid. We all get that these aren't legitimately low-cost productions. Ryan himself being on camera elevates the cost of the ad well beyond a small business budget. If you've ever *done* a green-screen based shoot, you know that the fact their lighting is perfectly on-point means they had a professional involved, their sound production is perfection, and even the post-production is immaculate. However, all of those pieces are not what makes their ads work, and you don't need them to take some lessons here. What makes their ads work is the authentic, down-to-earth humor of the scripts. It's the simple camera angles. It's using things that feel relevant to us, like a video that they clearly found online (and I will assume licensed properly), not shot by a professional, of a goat headbutting the camera operator.

The humor works for two reasons:

1. Ryan's delivery is on point - he pauses when he needs to, speeds up when he needs to, and holds eye contact with the camera in a way that feels like he's talking to you directly.

2. It catches you off guard - he's not afraid to grab the thing that is a little weird ("They put their names on arenas, we put our name [pause] on my lower back").

Those scripts can take a moment to land on and refine. If you're going to aim for incorporating humor, I highly recommend taking some comedy classes, or at least testing your jokes out on a few people before you release them to the wider world. Remember that most comedians release only a fraction of the jokes they come up with. Just because Ryan makes it look effortless doesn't mean it always is. He's also had a lot of time to perfect that sense of humor. So cut yourself some slack if it's not hilarious right out the gate.

This section's creativity spark prompt is going to be slightly different than the last because we're going to break it into two parts.

First, analyze how Mint Mobile shows their message of "low cost". What inspiration can you take from the low-budget, low-effort appearance of their ads to use in your own marketing?

Secondly, where and how can you use humor in your own marketing? What style of humor do you want to pattern after? Can you think of a comedian or two that you'd like to mimic? What is it about their style that works for them and that you want to mimic?

The BPS Example

Glen Bhimani runs BPS Security, headquartered in my hometown of San Antonio, TX. In an industry that is frequently in the news in some capacity or another for failures to perform, Glen is committed to upholding a higher standard. He has automated every possible aspect of the BPS back office. This ensures that not only is technology holding his guards accountable to perform their assigned duties and rounds on-time, but he receives automated reporting, licensing reminders, and so much more. He's running a massive security firm, better than most, with a fraction of the administrative staff. This allows him to pay his guards better *and* still be on-par or cheaper than the majority of his competition (at least, out of the companies that actually *pay* their guards, but that's a completely different issue[9]).

That aside, this is supposed to be about their marketing! And Glen faces a classic challenge here. Everyone, not just in the security industry, likes to use, "We're different from the competition!" as their marketing message. Glen probably has a better excuse to use it than most. The problem is when everyone is saying "We're better than the competition," it quickly becomes just another one in the crowd and the unconscious message is that you're just like the rest. While BPS could tackle things from the perspective of what they actually *do* do differently, the messaging is still going to fade into the marketplace. Instead their message is about how they are upholding a higher standard for the entire industry and they focus intently on showing that.

---

9 Before I met Glen, I was under the impression that the security industry was tightly buttoned up. Guards are often armed and responsible for ensuring that property and people are safe. In theory, they are held to continuing education, licensing, insurance standards, and more. In theory. The truth is the licensing requirements aren't the tightest. Continuing education standards are thin. Few companies uphold equipment standards and most require the guards to provide their own armaments. Worst of it all, it's a surprisingly common practice to simply not pay the security guards themselves for their work or to pay only marginally better than minimum wage. It is a high-turnover industry with a lot of burnout due to guards working multiple jobs. It's disturbing to say the least.

How do they do it? They actively call-out the insanity in the industry both with funny sketches and short videos, but also with actual calls to action to lawmakers and fellow security professionals. They have had numerous TV and press requests and appearances to discuss their practical approaches to security in regards to industry-related news. Most importantly, since a piece of their messaging hints that most of the rest of the industry is a bit of a joke, they take a more whimsical stance with their marketing and aren't afraid to film some crazily hilarious short sketches to put out there. In one of my favorite of their videos, Glen is shown trying to go about his regular day activities. Everything he tries to do however is hampered by his guards getting in his way while trying to protect him. As he reaches for the door to his house, his guard jumps in the way, opening the door a crack and peering out to ensure there's nothing out there. As Glen tries to get into his car, two guards jump in his way to open the door and cautiously check the interior. As he goes to get his mail, it turns into a slapping match as his guards push him away. The last shot is an image of the two guards who have been getting in his way sitting on the curb, heads down as Glen gently chides them that "Guys, this isn't what I meant when I said we have our client's backs 24/7!"

And it pays off. Despite having a relatively small online following, BPS Security generates thousands and thousands of views on their videos and was one of the fastest growing security firms in the US in 2020.

On the off chance that your marketing message sounds pretty darn similar to most of your competition[10], how can the BPS Security example inspire you to show it differently? Jot down some ideas here:

---

10   Note that if your message is "We're better than our competition" or "we care more" or any iteration of the above, you probably need to find a new angle to play with. You will *not* stand out from the crowd with this.

The Money P.I. Example:

Tanya has been working in medical billing for a long, long time. She's one of the best out there at understanding how coding needs to happen to ensure your medical practice is getting all of the money you're due from insurance. She understands where billing falls through the cracks, is filed incorrectly (or not at all), and where revenue gets lost. She's brilliant at digging in to find where you're leaking revenue and literally leaving dollars behind. But it was never her passion. No, Tanya lights up when her clients light up and realize where on earth their money is hiding. It took a few iterations to find, but in 2022 she finally opened The Money P.I., a coaching and training firm focused on helping everyday people figure out, as she puts it, "Where the F is my money?" In this business, Tanya works one-on-one and in small groups with the people who, on paper, should be fine and yet are constantly robbing Peter to pay Paul. Whether these are entrepreneurs, doctors, or working moms and dads who just want to be more stable financially, The Money P.I. is there.

Her brand is absolutely brilliant. The visuals are on-point with what she does and she embraces the brand wholeheartedly. She uses magnifying glasses, silhouettes, Sherlock Holmes-esque hats, and verbiage that revolves around investigate, private eye, etc. To break the ice while networking, her and I worked together to design the perfect piece. We crafted a fairly basic index card, but the text on the card is just a little too small to read easily. Then she'll whip out a cute little magnifying glass as a gift that makes it easy to read the font as it snakes its way around footprints that run across the card. Following the text reads: "It's easy to follow the trail to find missing money when you know what you need to investigate for! I'd love to help if you ever need it! Sincerely, the Money P.I." Talk about Show-Don't-Tell. She literally is the person to give them the tools to 'investigate' her brand.

If I have my way, I'll eventually convince her to do her own "Old Timey P.I." video. Picture it: Tanya in silhouette, feet up at a desk, smoking a bubble pipe in sepia. A dramatic woman flings herself into the room as the voiceover snarks in the classic, gumshoe chew: "She slunk into my office one dark and rainy evening.

You could tell she was in trouble from the way her eyes darted around the room. I wasn't a fan of trouble, but it had a way of finding me. I didn't do much with drama, but she was a dame in trouble. And I was here for it." These videos will be a truly hilarious and on-brand ways of telling the stories that Tanya has been able to help out with, in a way that makes it interesting to watch!

At the moment, Tanya is more into writing for her marketing than videos, but give me time and I'll warm her up!

What kinds of built-in visuals do you have for your brand? Can you use some kind of animal that really represents your core values? What about some variety of common household object like a magnifying glass for 'finding' or a laundry machine for cleaning, maybe a lamp for shedding light on something? Start by identifying what you want to showcase, and picking an object you can make part of your brand to showcase it! Like how my violins represent creativity and expertise at a glance!

The Dollar Shave Club Example

I spent years berating myself that my business didn't grow as quickly as Michael Dubin's Dollar Shave Club. The guy went from unknown (at least to me) to being a major player running a billion-dollar company in a matter of years. It was unprecedented. I've learned a lot since then. But I've also spent a lot of time evaluating that commercial that was such a big part of their overnight explosion.

If you aren't sure what I'm talking about, run a search on YouTube for "Dollar Shave Club Commercial" - it's the first one that comes up. In the commercial, Michael is walking through the warehouse, talking to the camera in the most casual manner. He walks through doors, drops some F-bombs, has a deadpan dry humor that keeps you chuckling, and in a little over 90-seconds, he drives home a lot of points:

1. You don't need a fancy blade - you just need a sharp one
2. Remembering to get your blades takes time and energy you don't have
3. These blades are cheap
4. These blades are great quality

Let's talk about *how* he does all this in 92 seconds while reiterating his point multiple ways!

First, how does he both manage to show that his blades are cheap and great at the same time? One of the most powerful things that happens in that commercial is the very simple warehouse backdrop. It feels accessible. There's a comfortable clutter to the background of the office that feels familiar and old-timey. It's got the desk we've all seen, at least in movies. The warehouse looks exactly like we expect. It feels like every other warehouse we've ever seen. The concept of a warehouse that is suck in the 80s by the looks of the wood paneled office feels cheap. It's not slick. It's not fancy. It's practical. We get the feeling that they are not wasting overhead on fancy spaces. At the same time, the commercial itself is polished, perfectly put together, easy to watch, funny, and makes sense. That is what gives it the sense of greatness. His deadpan delivery is on-point. The jokes keep coming right at the exact moment to keep you engaged. It's a 90-second commercial that you keep watching because you just want to know what's happening next. And the camera quality and audio is on-point. All that underpins the promise of cheap *and* great quality.

Next up, he promises that you don't need a fancy blade, just a sharp one. The commercial isn't fancy. But it is sharp with its humor. He talks about how you don't have time to remember to go get a new blade all the time and there is something about his delivery that also feels a little lazy. Not necessarily in a bad way – just in a "not gonna waste energy" way. Finally, they fit a *lot* of information into one 92 second commercial. Reinforcing that you don't have to spend time to get things done.

It's a short, powerful example of "show-don't-tell." I love it!

The Savannah Bananas Example

If you ask Jesse Cole, he'll tell you that the Savannah Bananas don't have a
marketing budget. To be fair, their ad-spend *is* $0. Knowing that, it seems a little
strange to talk about them inside of a marketing book. But since this *is* a book
on budget friendly marketing, and they are probably the epitome of success on
a budget, I think it makes sense. Because the truth is, they invest a lot of time in
how to live and breathe their marketing message. In fact, they might be one of the
best examples of Show-Don't-Tell I've ever experienced. They are certainly one I
endeavor to live up to.

I had the opportunity to attend a Savannah Bananas game in March 2022.
We were bringing Jesse in as the celebrity guest at our Fall 2022 Growcation
and as part of it, we arranged for all of our guests and staff to receive tickets to a
game[11]. We got our tickets through the main office and the moment I purchased
the tickets, my inbox lit up with a video from the Bananas. In it, the Bananas
alerted me that the moment the ticket was purchased, the entire team broke into

---

11   I think it's fair to add that, this was right before their ESPN special aired and a million+ person
waiting list and world tour, so it was a slightly different time for them!

cheers! I got to watch an obviously stylized version of what happened when two banana-shaped tickets were taken carefully out of a drawer, placed on a fluffy pillow, and raised to the light Lion King style. Confetti flew, team members danced, and they carefully packaged them in an envelope. It was hilarious!

When we got closer to the date of our game, I received a few emails!

One had a "Pre-Game Playlist" for us to listen to as we drove to the game.

Another had a "I'll be going Bananas" work-pass to fill out and send to your boss to be exempted from work the day of the game (which I dutifully sent to my team members, and they promptly filled out and turned in to me!).

Another had details about the game and what to expect. One point they made was that, since the stadium is first-come-first-serve for seating, lines start forming around 5:30 (for a game that starts at 7:30). Accordingly, we planned to arrive around 5:15 to be towards the start of the line. By the time we got onsite, the lines were already going! We got in line at least somewhere near the gates and snapped plenty of pictures with the banana bug van (an old Volkswagen van, painted up and parked near the entrance). It was raining, but no one in line really cared. Bananas staff were running through the crowd every so often to check in with the fans. Everyone waiting in line was ecstatic for the game. Right at gate-open time, a big brass band struck up. Before we knew what was happening, the entire team and a parade of gone-bananas people were dancing their way past us. The players ran between the lines, high-fiving and dancing like crazy people. When they saw the cameras we were holding up excitedly, they went, well, bananas.

Throughout the course of the game, we ordered two Garbage Can Nachos (Literally a giant metal lid with a ton of chips, cheese and accoutrement on top. Of course, with a banana on the side). We got pictures of all of them. We took about a hundred photos and clips of the game and the shenanigans that took place on the field. At one point, Split (their mascot) brought a sled up to the top of the stands, and rode it down the stands (after appropriately revving up the crowd).

And that, my friends, is a *fraction* of what it's like to experience the Savannah Bananas.

Why do I tell you all this?

The Savannah Bananas promise that "This is the greatest show in sports." This is a baseball experience, not a game. Their message is that they put fans first, always. They put fans first when they look at how to entertain throughout the entire game, from line-up to final bow. They've found every possible way to live the message that this is a show dedicated to *you*: the fan. In 2021, they made the decision to completely eliminate ads from their field in service of the ultimate fan experience. They pay the taxes on each ticket so that you are paying a flat fee. That flat, under $50 fee includes unlimited food and drink per person and admission to the game. Why? Because it's not Fans First if the fans are feeling taken for a ride by the time they finish buying $90 worth of food and walk away with nachos and a beer. The Bananas live to entertain, because they understand that is how they put the fans first. That is their promise. That is their message.

By the time the 90-minute game was finished, I was truly sad to realize it was over. I had (and still have) no real idea how baseball is played. But I had a blast. I wasn't the only person either. Every fan in the stands was taking photos and videos and posting them online.

The Bananas do plenty of their own documentation and sharing of their antics online. But what gets you at a Savannah Bananas game isn't necessarily when Jesse runs through the crowd in search of the right person to gift a rose to (and chooses the most adorable little girl who accepts the rose with equal parts bashfulness and excitement). It's not necessarily the banana branded drains around the stadium that most people wouldn't even notice. It's the hilarious signs telling you where to go that make it easy to feel right at home. It's the way the players keep the game going. As do the Banana Nanas (their grandma dance team) and their Dad Bod Cheerleading Squad. It's the enthused atmosphere that takes over even on a rainy night in Savannah, GA in March.

They promise that their game will be an experience. That it will be fun. And in order to ensure it's fun, they make it easy. They live up every moment of the game with you. Not only do they generate an insane amount of User Generated Content (UGC) from their antics, but even the videos and messages they push out embrace the theme of entertainment.

So yes. Jesse is right. Their marketing budget may be $0. But they don't shirk on investing in higher quality micro elements that surprise and thrill their audience. Because you have to believe that the mats in the bathroom spark a laugh, and pictures. The drains, for the few people who notice them, get photographed. The band and players running through the crowd, get photographed and shared. When the brass band leader autographs my sister's cheek because it just lives up to being *that* goofy, it gets posted online. Jesse and his team have embraced their message of fans first, entertain always. They do it through the big things, but they also do it through the small things. And that commitment to their message takes care of their marketing for them.

Jesse's books, *Find Your Yellow Tux* and *Fans First*, are well worth the read for a million more ideas of how to Show-Don't-Tell. I can't recommend them enough as your next stop.

What are two small ways you can show your message? Even if they are so small that no one else may notice? Like changing the drains around your stadium, or giving out fidget toys at an event for ADHD entrepreneurs, or ensuring that every video that goes out about your company is fun to back the message?

Fantastic! Just in case you haven't figured it out by now, take the ideas you've written down over the past few pages, type them up, and that list inside your Marketing folder!

The Methods of Distribution

"Hallelujah!" I hear you saying, "She's finally going to talk tactics!" I get it, it's taken a while to get to this point. I want to reassure you that figuring out *who* your target market is and *what* your message is will be the most time-consuming part of building a marketing plan. Honestly, once you know your Market and Message, the Methods are easy. Seriously – I spent less than an hour pulling together the marketing plan for the song *Fly – An Entrepreneur's Journey* on one lazy Saturday morning. Not only that, but it's easy to start getting creative with how you tackle it so you can stand out from the crowd when you have the framework of the first two Ms.

A word of warning. If we shirk the first two steps in our eagerness to get to the methods of distribution, it will be both harder to build a creative and unique strategy set and more likely that those tactics won't work. These two *are* the framework to how creativity can happen, just like color theory is the framework that creates great art. Trust me, I've been painting and drawing since I was a kid. I hated how they always looked cartoonish and off. In 2018, a coach suggested I do some study of color theory. It changed everything in my art. I'm no DaVinci, never will be. But my art is cohesive. The colors play off each other to highlight each other. I actually can hang some of my own art now and not hate it every time I walk by. So on the off chance you've been reading ahead, planning to just get to the end and get my best ideas to market your business, stop. Go back. Do the homework first. This next part won't work if you skipped the first two.

This is about to sound redundant, but bear with me because the number of times I get to the end of a training and someone walks up to me to ask, "Just real quick Steph, how should I market my business? I do _____" is a big mind-boggling. It's almost always someone who has been sitting in the audience taking notes, but you can tell that they were preoccupied during the training. Usually because they are worried about what to do to grow their business. The problem is that, while I love doing 15-minute creative marketing brainstorm sessions, I can't do that with a line of people waiting to talk to me, and with no real information. If I'm going to be able to get creative and come up with something that hasn't been done a hundred times before, I need some basic information like the target market details and an emotion-based marketing message. Otherwise, I'm just throwing out some basic ideas that probably won't generate the kind of impact the individual is looking for.

In these situations, because I'm a bit of a sucker to help others, I always back up the conversation and ask who their target market is. In most situations, we'll spend a couple of minutes identifying some distinct markers that make their audience unique and I'll encourage them to go do more research to find out where that unique audience lives online and off. If they have a solid idea of their target market already, the next question is always "What is the message?" In the conversations that get this far, nine times out of ten, the message they are trying to communicate is the same one being used by 95% of their industry. Usually some iteration of "We do things better than the competition." And I understand that identifying your marketing message is not easy. But unless your marketing message stands out, your marketing won't either. And if your marketing doesn't stand out, it's not going to work. I can't pull creative ideas out of thin air. I need some framework to work within! So do you.

I hope that this is enough encouragement for you to go back and make sure that your marketing message is unique and evocative.

If you've followed the instructions but you're still not sure, check out MarketingBeyondSocialMedia.com – I'll make sure that page always has some kind of resource that will give you space to share your marketing message and get feedback! Once you have that, make sure you take time to come up with your own list of ways to Show-Don't-Tell. Double check that you've got the target market researched and defined, and know that the next part of this process is the FUN part!

Let's go!

Despite this usually being the shortest portion of my training, I'm going to take a minute to break it down here in a little more detail for you. While it's the easiest part of the plan building (as long as you've done the previous two steps!), it's also the practical and tangible part that everyone needs the most. So we're going to dig deep here! There are three really important documents you'll want to put together for your Methods of Distribution. These are the pieces that you'll actually focus on executing with the last one being the most important they are:

1. The Ideal Conversion Process
2. The Project Plan
3. The Baseline

Let's get started.

The Ideal Conversion Process

I'm going to drop two words here in a second, I want you to keep reading. I know that these two words have been misused and abused. They've been used as ways to manipulate people into buying stuff they don't need. They've been over-complicated a million different ways and become synonymous with some software out there that you do *not* need to buy to do this well. So relax, I'll walk you through it step by step!

This is your *customer journey* or *sales funnel*. Not a one-click-funnel or a series of contrived landing pages that take someone from ad-viewer to product-buyer. But the laid-out process by which someone would convert to buy from you, and then buy again and again and again. Because we all know that the lifetime value of a client is one of the most critical things to increase if we want to grow our businesses. It is the most affordable way to generate revenue. Getting someone to buy from you again and again is one of the most important parts of how business gets easier the longer you stay in business.

But! Understanding how your new clients get from not even knowing you exist to considering buying from you, then making the decision to buy from you, and joining the fold (so to speak) is a critical part to understanding your marketing strategy. This is what will influence where you put your 'hooks' or brand exposure points to get their attention. It will influence how you lay out your website. It will also influence how you adjust each step of the process to ensure that your prospect is receiving all of the information that they need to feel comfortable making a buying decision.

I've sat through a lot of painful classes on how to do this so I'm going to try to make this as easy as possible. Let's document your conversion process together. Treat this section especially like a workbook for yourself if you want to get the most out of it.

Start by identifying all of the ways that someone might find out about your business. These are your 'hooks' or brand exposure points. For example, for Grow Disrupt it's:

1. I speak on stage and they are in the audience.

2. They see either my or our brand social media content – usually on my page or because it was shared by a friend.

3. Social content gets picked up by the algorithm and circulates to new audiences.

4. They find one of our websites, articles, or videos online either through online placements or search engine optimization.

5. We're featured by a joint-marketing partner in a blog, newsletter, podcast, video, etc – and they are in that audience and resonate with what they see.

6. They read an article that I'm featured in on another website.

7. I'm featured in a news segment and they see the live airing or see the replay on a site they frequent (or that gets shared by a friend on social media).

8. They grabbed a copy of this book from seeing it online, in a listing, or at a bookstore.

9. They grabbed a copy of any of the other books that I've been featured.

10. A friend literally tells them about us.

At this point in time, we don't do billboards, TV or radio ads, or any other major traditional marketing. So these are pretty much the primary ways that someone will find us.

Take a minute and list out all the ways that someone might encounter your brand:

1.
2.
3.
4.
5.
6.
7.
8.

Excellent! Nicely done.

When I first started building customer journeys, this is where I'd spiral. Each of these introduction-points to the brand might not result in the exact same brand discovery process. For example, if someone has just barely found one of our articles, they may not even consider checking out the remainder of the website. Just because they found us featured on another site doesn't mean they will come to our site and if they do, they might not all come to the same page. And the same thing goes if they see some of our social media.

I'm not kidding when I say I spent days and days with too many mind maps scrawled on massive sheets of paper, spread across the floor of my office, trying to figure out the exact process every single person might follow. My goal was to better understand how every person found the brand so we could maximize the number of people who warmed up to the brand and went on to the next step in the funnel.

It was far from helpful.

So to save you a little angst, let's skip that part.

You don't need to understand every single possible path. You need to understand what would be a good indicator that someone would be warming up to the brand and considering buying so you can actively try to drive people to that step. I call this the Brand Engagement Indicator. For Grow Disrupt it's when they visit the *Our Difference* page on our website. This is the page that lays out how our events are different from the industry and a little bit of how they are made for people with ADHD. If someone goes to this page, it's because they want to learn about Grow Disrupt and have questions about our events. If they make it to that page, and click one of the options on that page, I know they are a prospect worth putting my time and energy (and maybe some money) into.

Keep in mind, as you get all these pieces of your marketing going, you're going to have plenty of people who will find out about your brand but it won't really register or they just aren't a fit. All you have to do is offer them the option to go to the next stage in the 'courtship' of waking up to your brand. You're never going to convert everyone. You don't want to.

So for now, let's focus on the people who *are* a fit for your brand.

What is your *Our Difference* page? What action do they take (before they reach out to you or try to book with you) that tells you they are seriously considering working with you? In today's day and age, there's a pretty good chance it's something on your website. Do they visit a second product page? Do they go to the About page? If you're in retail or selling direct to consumer, do they go to your social media? For example, if you're a restaurant, they might go to your social media to look for pictures of the food or menu before driving across town to try you out. You get to decide, right now, where you want to direct people once they have a brand exposure to warm them up enough to contact you.

Take a minute and write down what step people either already take, or you want them to take when they first engage with your brand seriously.

The next step should be the initial contact. This could go one of two ways depending on whether you've got a sales team to close the deal or you're trying to draw them towards the sale directly. As a good rule of thumb, if you've got a hefty price tag associated with your sale, or enough options that the buyer might need a trained expert to help navigate their selection, you'll want to get them transitioned to the sales team or individual. Brick-and-mortar businesses (retail or restaurants) who need to get their customers to show up in-person or businesses that are trying to drive sales online with no interaction are going to start drawing the prospect towards the sale itself right now.

If you want them to make contact before they start moving towards the sale so you can transition them to a salesperson, now's the time to identify that *and* how they are most likely to do so. Will they call the office? Will they fill out a form on the website? Open the chat? Book an appointment on the website for a consult? What do you want them to do so you can transition them to your sales team?

As an important note, once you've got first contact, plan to pull them into your brand ecosystem so you can keep building exposure and trust with your brand The brand ecosystem is all the things you do to re-market to someone after the initial brand exposure. This can be inviting them to follow you on Social Media, or adding them to your emailing list. If you are feeling particularly adventurous, look into how to set up a series of emails to go out automatically from your emailing platform once they sign up. These emails should introduce them to the key aspects of your brand, like your message, mission, team, and product or service.

If you are brick-and-mortar (retail or restaurants usually), or just looking for them to check-out online, start by asking yourself what's the next step that they *should* take once they start thinking about buying from you? Do they download the menu? Make a reservation? Go to your social media to look at photos? Call the store to see if you have what they are looking for in stock? Start putting things in the cart so they can check how much shipping would be? Open the chat and fill out the contact info to talk to a real person? I'm sure there are a variety of ways they can make the initial contact. Your job is to pick the one you think is best right now. All roads will need to drive there. The other options can exist, but whatever you want them to do most, your life will be a lot easier if you decide that now. You're welcome to change it down the road but, for now, pick *one* and stick with it.

Take a minute to think. In an ideal world, how would you have people let you know when they are getting serious? Write it down.

I know this can feel a little heavy, so for a quick recap, there are three steps you should have documented by now:

The Brand Exposure Points
The Brand Engagement Indicator
The Initial Contact Method

If you're feeling particularly inspired and want this organized, type up the answers you've jotted down into a single document. Name it "My Customer Conversion Process" and save it in that folder next to your marketing message and your target market research.

If you have a sales team or person, the heavy lifting for marketing is usually over at this point. You can still send the prospective customer emails and hope they see your social media to stay warm to the brand, but most of the weight is on the sales team at this point.

If this is you, and you'd like, you can skip ahead to the **Bolded Header**. If you are in a business where they will make most of the buying decision without talking to anyone, there's a little more work to do here.

If your first purchase is going to happen without them talking to you first, you need to identify one more step in the process: The First Purchase (i.e. what they are most likely to buy). What is your entry product? This is the product you put front and center on the website, in your marketing, etc. If you have a few, great. But try to identify the top few products that draw people to your website because you'll want to put the most effort into making sure these products are set up enticingly enough to get put in the cart.

For example, on TheStephanieScheller.com we have two products: The Done-For-You Marketing Plan and the Marketing Spark Labs. Both of these can be purchased separately and without any conversation with a member of my team. They are both inexpensive enough that conversions can happen without me having to get involved personally to close the deal. Between the two, more people will buy the Done-For-You Marketing Plan first. It's incredibly affordable. Simple. Easy to implement. It makes sense. And frankly, it makes more sense to do a Spark Lab if you've got a marketing plan in place. So all roads point to the plan first and we've put a lot of time into adjusting the page to entice people to click to the check-out page.

 Write down your First Purchase here:

The Bolded Header (I.e. Start reading here if you were skipping ahead)

The last part of the conversion process is easy in theory and challenging in application. It's time to make sure the right information is in the right places. Based on your target market research, what information is your ideal buyer going to want before they will be comfortable either moving into the initial contact, or purchasing your product without a conversation? Make a list of this information, then lay out where to put this information in a way that it will be easy to find for the prospective customer.

If they are going to want testimonials, how can you thread those throughout the product page or every page on the website because, trust me, no one is building trust from a testimonials page that no one visits? If they are going to want product specifications, make sure they are easy to find. If they want your menu, ensure they can find and read it easily. If they are going to want to check out your social media for some social proof or pictures of your food, make it easy to get there (and back). Better yet, embed a live stream of your most recent posts on the website if possible.

The most important piece of all this is that knowing the ideal process that I want the customer to go through allows me to focus just on getting the customer to the next stage. In our Initial Contact, my only goal is to get them to check out the website. Once they get to the website, my only goal is to get them to the brand engagement indicator. From there, I can focus on how to get them into the initial contact.

When we have that kind of clarity with our marketing, we can be concise. We can position ourselves as the expert. We can make a big impact.

Make a list now of
1) what information your prospect needs in order to move to the next stage and
2) where to put it on your website in your conversion process document now.

The Project Plan

Time for step two. This one is always fun!

A quick heads up to make your life easier: The more detailed you make the project plan as you're building it, the easier it will be to implement, and therefore the more likely you are *to* implement. The more corners you cut now and the more vague you make this, the harder it will be down the road. So when I push you to document more details *now* while you're in planning mode, take advantage of it. This isn't me being difficult. It's me trying to be nice!

In short, the project plan is a list of all the activities that need to be completed to deploy your brand new marketing message across all your assets and kick off your new, cohesive marketing strategy. It is all of the one-and-done assignments. This could be:

- Overhauling your brand or website
- Building a landing page
- Creating outbound content (emails or social posts) for the kick-off
- Designing a flier
- Getting promotional material ordered
- Registering on certain listing websites
- Getting graphics put together for a billboard
- Commissioning a jingle or an animated clip of your brand to use in your marketing videos
- Researching influential partners to start building relationships with
- [Insert More Here]

If you're kicking off a marketing plan to try and recruit more employees, you may build a project plan that just focuses on what activities you need to knock out to get all the pieces off the ground. That may include writing the job ad, identifying platforms to put it up on, getting videos from current employees to share, etc.

If you're just looking to kick off a micro-marketing campaign to promote a single thing inside of your overall marketing plan this may only be a page or two long. For example, the plan I built for *Fly – An Entrepreneur's Journey* had a project plan that was only a page and a half. However, if this is the project plan to kick off your overall marketing plan and you're overhauling an entire department and a lot of assets[12], this document may be several pages long.

If you're overhauling your entire marketing strategy with a lot of moving pieces, your project plan may cover updating all of your existing marketing assets as well as deploying new strategies. If it's the latter, expect for it to take a few months for your project plan to be fully implemented. That's ok! In my experience, it's better to get things done slowly over time than try and set it all up for one big launch. The only things I might encourage you to roll out all at once would be a new brand across all visual elements like your website, fliers, business cards, etc. Otherwise, the other items we're going to talk about putting on your project plan can be rolled out piece by piece over however much time as you need. One of the biggest mistakes you can make here is trying to keep a project plan intended to overhaul your entire brand short enough to implement overnight or beating yourself up for not getting it done that fast.

Before you get overwhelmed, I'm going to walk you through, step-by-step, how to build your project plan but first, an example.

Capri Temporary Housing:

Capri Temporary Housing is a corporate housing provider that leases and furnishes apartments in cities across much of the Southwestern United States. They then re-lease these furnished apartments to individuals who are traveling for work. These people will typically be in an area for long enough to make hotel living a drain, and short enough for buying a home or signing a lease to make little sense. Anna, the owner and founder (and for transparency's sake, also my mother!) started Capri back in 2011 when she saw the need in our hometown of Del Rio, TX. Del Rio is a tiny little town on the Texas-Mexico border and Anna ran a solid multi-six-figure business steadily for years. Then in 2021, a lot of the lessons she'd been learning over the years, on her own and while working with me at our events, came together. She made some extremely smart decisions, and the business blew up. Capri's revenue literally 10x'd in a single year. There were some major growing pains along the way. One of which was their marketing. What worked back when it was a home-based business that was as much about keeping us kids employed over the summers as it was about making money was no longer that same business. While Anna was killing it in the sales arena and had landed some major contracts to facilitate that growth, their marketing was

---

12   I use this term with relative frequency and I don't even know if it's industry jargon anymore or just a phrase I landed on to encompass all of the pieces that represent your brand. Social media channels. Websites. Fliers. Business cards. Handouts. Basically, all of the things that help you market your business? They are your marketing assets!

not keeping up. The logo reflected the size of the business when it was created back in the early 2010s and their marketing strategy mostly included a website and some pretty empty social media channels. Anna was increasingly feeling the need to build marketing that would attract additional major clients and started to reach out for suggestions and help.

The first thing we did was sit down to conduct some detailed research of the target markets that would be making the buying decisions. These are primarily HR and Procurement directors and we ended up with twenty-six pages of research on these guys and gals. Then we inventoried everything that made Capri special and unique and built a marketing message that would appeal to the target market. More importantly, it was unique to Capri and Anna's strengths and personalities and would stand out instantly in an industry that can feel sterile and austere. Even better, it gave us lots of evocative, emotional fodder.

I already knew this from having grown up with her, but Anna's strong Italian heritage is one of their greatest assets when it comes to the hospitality industry. Italian hospitality is legendary! Tell me you can't instantly picture a little old Nonna, wrapped in her apron, at the stove, cutting herbs and stirring a big pot of pasta sauce. She turns from the stove to look at you and, fingers pressed together in that classic Italian movement, she waggles her hand at you. Her eyes crinkle as she asks "Why you looka so skinny? Are you not eating? Eat! Mangiare!" I mean, that's literally my Nonna in my head. But it's a pretty classic image we've seen on a hundred TV shows and in marketing for places like Olive Garden. The world knows what is meant by Italian Hospitality.

Knowing that about the hospitality industry, and Anna, we built her a marketing message that revolved around that heritage and instant emotional connection. Her new message (summed up) became, "A taste of Italian Hospitality in the Corporate Housing industry." Unlike hotels that leave you feeling cramped, eating out constantly, and with nowhere comfortable to relax during your down-time, a Capri apartment is a taste of that laid-back Italian country life. As Anna promises, "You won't want to go home!"

Message decided and target market researched, it was time to start asking ourselves how we could Show-Don't-Tell this message. We started jotting down ideas. Some of them were a little wild (Have an Italian grandma bring them dinner their first night in a Capri apartment!). Some were a little more reasonable (craft a custom recipe of dry ingredients in a jar to make Nonna's signature pasta sauce and provide a meal kit for their first night). Some were non-negotiable (refresh and update the branding). Once we had a list of ways we could show the message, we started building a list of all the ways we wanted to market Capri to support Anna's sales initiatives. Then it was time to start building our project plan.

The initial project plan was pretty comprehensive and took more than three months to complete the first phase. I'm including a truncated version at the bottom of this section of the book, Anna asked me not to release the entire thing since some projects are still in-the-works, but you can see some more sample project plans at MarketingBeyondSocialMedia.com.

Once we had the project plan, we got to work. We refreshed the branding[13], got a new website built, updated social media profiles along with fliers, handouts, and guest guides. We tested and finalized a recipe to bring the dry ingredients of Nonna's Signature Pasta Sauce into every Capri apartment. So when new guests arrive, one of the first things they see is pasta, a can of tomato sauce, a welcome card (with simple, easy-to-follow instructions) and a mason jar with a delicious compilation of the dry ingredients for legitimately Italian pasta sauce. We set up a CRM and outbound LinkedIn campaigns. We pulled together lists of PR contacts to run outbound PR campaigns and registered to represent Anna across a variety of PR platforms.

Notice how every single one of those is a "one and done" task? Refresh the company brand? Done! And once it's done, you don't need to do it again, at least not for awhile. Get a new website built? Done! And now, we can update the website and add landing pages, but we don't have to rebuild the whole website again for a while. Set up a CRM? Done. Set up an outbound LinkedIn campaign? Done. Pull together contacts? Done. Register on platforms? Done.

And before you panic, yes, there's ongoing work too…we'll talk about that in a minute when we get to the baseline.

As a quick preview in case your brain is panicking like I know mine would be right now: the baseline is a list of all the activities you'll be doing on a recurring basis. So you'd list on the baseline to "check PR platforms daily" and "send out LinkedIn messages to prospects daily" or however frequently you want to! I'll walk you through it when we get there so, take a deep breath, I've got your back.

To contrast that with a "micro-marketing campaign project plan" - we recently worked on how we would tackle an event that Capri was sponsoring. This was a short-term plan that just needed a project plan to execute, but that wouldn't require a baseline, or even a ton of extra project work to get done. Here's how we tackled that.

---

13 You can see their beautiful new, Italian-influenced branding at CapriHousing.com

First things first, we inventoried the budget and assets. This was a relatively last-minute event to add to the calendar, so by the time we finished paying for the sponsorship, we had about $500 left to spend on laying out the booth. Second, we knew that only Anna was available to attend the event itself. The last thing we wanted was to require her to stand at a booth for the entire event. Instead, we asked ourselves if we could build a booth that would draw people in to check it out, give them an idea of the company and the brand, and leave them wanting more. We decided to move forward with an idea we'd been noodling for a few weeks of "Teodoro the Tomato" and get a mascot created. We found tomato-shaped stress balls online and my graphic designer created an adorable mascot design. Our plan was to put the Teodoros in a wicker basket on the right side of the table. Over the basket would be a sign with a picture of a smiling Teodoro and an invitation to "Take One" along with a little card to introduce the little guy and all his personality! We then created three easy-to-read (think big font – minimal text) fliers that could be stood up in those plastic sleeves on the table (you know the ones I'm talking about). Anna also ordered a gingham tablecloth (think *Lady and The Tramp* dinner-in-the-alley style) to put on the table at an angle over the characteristic Capri blue base tablecloth. Teodoro would draw them in, then the fliers would tell a story and draw the viewer down through the booth with a QR code to get more info at the end.

Then, as usual, challenges arose. The tomatoes weren't going to arrive in time for the event! Instead of panicking, we found a sweet (literally) solution. I'd previously found an online cookie provider that could print a graphic on a cookie and have it shipped to you in just a matter of days. We had a cookie graphic of Teodoro created and ordered the cookies. We also ordered little burlap sacks, big enough for the cookie and the Meet Teodoro cards.

Then we had two more designs created. One flier was created to stand up next to the cookies with a picture of the Teodoro cookies, and an intro to our little Teo so people could see what was waiting for them and invite them in big letters to take a bag. The second design was a quarter-sheet card that explained what happened. A QR code in the bottom invited them to scan and input their info to get a jar of Nonna's Signature Pasta Sauce Starter and a real-life Teodoro to "make your day a little brighter!" once the tomatoes arrived. During the event, Anna was walking around networking with a few extra cookies in her bag and a few jars of the pasta sauce starter to give out whenever she found someone who fit her target market profile.

Ultimately, the event was a smash, Anna had prospects coming to seek her out and start conversations because they loved the book and, of course, request a

Teodoro and pasta sauce kit. At the end of it, we spent just under $500 (And that included our $277 tomatoes not arriving on time!).

Since we're talking about project plans, and specifically what a project plan for a micro-marketing campaign might look like versus a major marketing campaign, here's the difference between the overhaul project plan versus the event project plan:

Overhaul Project Plan

1. Rebrand company
2. Build new website
   a. Research core SEO phrases to built content around
   b. Ensure Analytics, Search Console, and a heatmap software are installed on the website
   c. Highlight executive features on home page
   d. Pages to include:
      I.   Home
      II. About Us
      III. Areas Served
      IV. Contact Us
      V.   Template landing page for cities you carry heavy loads of apartments in that can collect SEO rankings, but also be used for pay per click as needed to fill vacancies
   e. Create content
   f. Select photos
3. Update business cards
4. Update Social Media Profiles
   a. Twitter
   b. LinkedIn
   c. Facebook
5. Italian-Inspired Photo Shoot for custom stock photography
6. Layout, film & edit introductory video
   a. Starts with "horror" feel of staying at a hotel
   b. Transforms to warm, homey, welcoming when they "come home to Capri"
7. Update fliers (Complete with a list of which fliers to update)
8. Create fliers (Complete with a list of what to create, and what should be included)
9. Create "Nonna's Signature Pasta Sauce" starter kit & instruction cards

10. Create Standard Operating Procedure for Nonna's Signature Pasta Sauce
11. Set up CRM
12. Design outbound LinkedIn campaign scripts
13. Create list of PR contacts for outreach
14. Register on PR platforms (HARO, Qwoted, Sourcebottle)

(Keep in mind, this is a fraction of the full project plan I originally built for Capri! The original was five pages long. More detailed = better!!)

Event Project Plan:

After we decided exactly what we needed to do, our project plan looked a little something like this:

1. Get Teodoro created!
2. Get Teodoro ordered!
3. Create content for:
    a. Three 'story' fliers
    b. 'Take a Teodoro" flier
    c. Meet Teodoro Card
    d. *Added Later*: Invite to request Teodoro card
    e. *Added Later*: Create Teodoro Cookie Design
    f. *Added Later*: Landing page to request Teodoro & Pasta Sauce
4. Send off designs to:
    a. Web designer
    b. Graphic designer
5. Get printed material to local printer by [Friday before event]
6. Get gingham tablecloth ordered!
7. *Added Later*: Order burlap bags!
8. *Added Later*: Order cookies!

Build Your Own Project Plan:

So now it's time to build your own project plan. Remember: detailed is better. It's better to take time *now* to lay out what pages you want on the website, and what kind of content to put on the flier than waiting till later[14]. Now you're in strategy and "see the big picture" mode! Later, you may not be. So let yourself think about "Ok! We need to overhaul the website. What pages should we have to appeal to our target market? What sections should each page have? What

---

14 As a quick note in case you're getting ahead of me – you're not going to create the actual content here. Just the outlines. More on this later.

information did I uncover in the conversion process section that should be included? Where do I put it?" And write it down. Write as much as you possibly can. I'd leave space for you to do so here, but I don't want you limiting yourself to whatever space I can fit into this book.

So instead, go to that folder that you created to store your target market and marketing message, start a new document, and title it "Project Plan [Date]" and now it's time to go ham!

Start by creating a list in the project plan document of all the marketing assets you want to update or create.

This could even start with "Do I need to get a new/updated brand built out?" Or you could just list out all the fliers, business cards, websites, landing pages, radio ads, tv commercials, billboards, social media profiles, swag, and so-on that need to be updated or created to reflect the new marketing message or brand.

First: Get All Assets in Alignment

When I'm starting from scratch with building a marketing plan, I know that I first need to bring all the current marketing assets into alignment. I like checklists, so I create a list of all the assets to review first. Once I have a list of all the assets, I will put my computer in split-screen with the Message document on the left and the asset I'm auditing on the right. I typically swap the left side of the screen between the Message and the Project Plan documents to make notes in. This allows me to keep the message front of mind as I'm reviewing and make detailed notes on what needs to be updated for each asset.

The only exception to this formula is when I'm completely overhauling a website. Because that document can get lengthy on its own, I usually have a separate document just for website overhaul notes. This portion of the project plan alone can be 3-5 pages long. I will typically add a note in the project plan to "Update Website - See Notes in Website Project Plan" which is a document I will keep in the same folder with all the other files for this marketing plan. As a bonus, once I chose a web developer, now I just need to send them this document and any brand documents (brand guides and messaging docs) to get them going.

Pro Tip: When updating your website, make sure you have your webmaster add in Google Analytics, Search Console, and some variety of heatmap[15] software (see MarketingBeyondSocialMedia.com for my current preferred option). While you're at it, make sure that these are set up in *your* google account. I can't tell you the number of people who have lost years of data inside an analytics account because it was originally set up in the webmaster's google account and got lost or deleted during a transition. While you won't need these right away, they can start collecting data that you'll get into later and will appreciate having! If you're building your site for yourself on a template program like Wix, Square or Strikingly, you might need to ask their site support for help getting that installed. If it's causing frustration, move on. You can come back and add it later.

Last note here, this is great to have, but it's not worth getting stuck. If you can't figure it out relatively quickly, move on. You can add this later.

Let's go back to one of my earlier footnotes and elaborate a bit more. The project plan doesn't include the actual content. I will typically lay out what kind of content needs to be listed in an outline format, but I don't create the actual *content* during the audit. That's a different set of brain muscles! But if I'm listing that a flier needs to be updated I might list out something that looks like:

- Update Referral Partner Flier
  - Update logo & branding overall
  - Turn into a tri-fold flier
  - Should include info on:
    - Who we are
    - Why we are different
    - Why we value our partners
    - Why our partners refer to us
    - A few testimonials

It sounds kind of nuts to get that detailed, but it makes my life a lot easier. When I go to create the content for the flier before sending it off to the designer. Instead of asking myself "What should this flier focus on?" I've already got a list and instead I can focus on "What's the best, and most succinct way, to answer this question!" In the same way, a website plan might look like an overview of

---

15 A piece of software that is installed on your website and will track what visitors do when visiting the site to provide you with insights about where they click, how far down the page they visit before leaving and more. Note that these software do *not* tie this data to any particular site visitor so while you might need to add a note in your privacy policy, you are not really infringing on anyone's personal data.

each of the pages the website should have, and then a list of what sections to include on each page. But I won't necessarily stress about what exact text to put in each section during the audit. In fact, one line on the project plan is usually: "Create Content for Website/Fliers/Emails."

Ready? It's time to go audit your assets and start building your project plan. Go into your Project Plan document and review the list of assets you created and start making notes on what to update as you review each asset one-by-one.

Second: Brainstorm Tactics

Once I've finished listing out exactly what I need to do to get all of my marketing assets aligned, I can move to the next stage of building my project plan. Namely: What else should I be doing?

Look at the list of ways you came up with to Show-Don't-Tell, your marketing message and decide which ones you want to make a reality now. Review your target market and ask yourself, "What can I do with this information?" Most importantly, as you're compiling ideas in the next few steps, write them down on a scratch pad. No idea is a bad idea, just start somewhere for now, you'll organize it into the Project Plan document in a minute.

For example, do your people like to volunteer at the Food Bank? Do you know someone at the local Food Banks? Could you call them up and offer to sponsor a "Volunteer Refreshment Table" this weekend during their peak volunteer time? Ask if you could write a check for a couple hundred dollars if they will put a sign saying "Provided by [Your Company Name]" on the table with Gatorades and snacks (or even just bring the snacks yourself if they will let you!). Then show up and volunteer as well. If you're going to do this, don't forget to ask yourself how you can Show-Don't-Tell your message through that table. Can you come up with your own Teodoro to put out? Make sure it's something that is unique enough that everyone will actually want it, and that represents your message. Because as cool as those koozies are, unless your message has to do with "Staying cool longer" or "Keep the 'beer sweat' off your hand," they aren't doing you any major favors.

When faced with our own question of what to create to put out when I speak and around town for Grow Disrupt, we realized that ADHD entrepreneurs love stickers for some weird reason. So we designed a sticker, visual below, and got it printed up big and glossy and put those out. They're always gone by the time I get back to my table whenever I'm at an event because they speak to my audience and make them feel empowered for what makes them unique.

Once you've gone through your target market line-by-line and asked "Is there some way I can use this information?" for every single line, it's time to go back to our trusty friend: Google. I'm just looking for inspiration at this point, so I'll start with a search that looks like "Ways to Market [my industry]." Usually what results is pages and pages of listacles. I like to open as many as my computer can handle (usually fifteen to twenty tabs at once if I'm being honest). Then I close the search tab and start reading. Every time I get an idea that I like, I write it down. Sometimes those ideas are directly pulled from the article. Most of the time, they are inspired by that article.

For example, this is where I got the idea for the mini experience boxes for the 2022 Growcation. The article I was reading was talking about how swag is a great way to market. But I didn't need to market to the people at the event (which is when I'd typically lean on swag!). Because I've been tuning and sharpening my creativity muscle however, my brain asked if I could send some swag in advance.

At this point, I dove down the rabbit hole with reckless abandon. I spent a solid few minutes first arguing with myself that the swag we use for the Growcation is quite expensive. I'd destroy margins and cheapen the actual onsite experience if everyone who said they wanted to go, got some of that swag before the event even happened. I wasn't interested in buying a bunch of cheap, giveaway-style swag either. As we've discussed, the Growcation is a luxury brand. I can't promise luxury, then send crappy pens and basic swag. So, out came the scratch paper. I started by asking myself, "What *could* I send them that would feel special, unique, luxurious, and quintessentially Bananas?" (remember, our guest was Jesse Cole of the Savannah Bananas!). I started with, "I could send Banana bread" then asked, "Ok, but how do I elevate it so it feels special?" And that's the short version of how we landed on toasted oat, cinnamon and rum banana bread with a tiny banana shaped stress toy and a handwritten note.

I don't share all of this just for the sake of seeing words on the page. I'm sharing this so you can see a little bit of what it's like to actually go through this - even for me. As I talked about at the beginning, we often see the violinist drawing music from the instrument so gracefully that it's intimidating. Or we see the final product of the marketing campaign and think "Wow! That was so creative. I could never do something like that." But trust me, there's a lot of doubt, questioning, and really dumb ideas that either never saw the light of day, or were absolute duds when we released them! For example, the Thor City video that my team and I spent months crafting, filming, editing and releasing. A video that racked up a grand total of two views on the first launch.

There will be duds and there will be ideas that will be wholly impractical.

Keep going. The gem is around the corner.

Once you've gone through the listacles from our favorite online content collector and started to compile your own list of ideas, now you can start to prioritize your list of marketing ideas. Start by looking for which ones best represent the message. Then ask yourself which of these ideas you're most excited about. Anything that doesn't spark excitement for me doesn't get onto the project plan. I recommend you adopt the same philosophy. Those that *do* get organized into action steps to kick off their implementation, then added to the Project Plan document. For example, if I've decided that I want to run a PR campaign, I might break the kick-off down into the following action steps:

Research local journalists and media sources who focus on [my industry] - compile into spreadsheet with email addresses

Connect with journalists and media sources on LinkedIn and Twitter

Create first pitch and email it out

At this point, your project plan should probably be a few pages long if this is your initial marketing plan!

Go deep.

You won't regret it later! I promise.

IF YOU HAVEN'T ALREADY, NOW IS A GOOD TIME TO GO:

1. Plan out how to get your assets in alignment.
2. Review the Target market for ideas.
3. Research and brainstorm ideas online.
4. Build your project plan of one-and-done ideas for updating the brand and kicking off your new marketing tactics.

Remember – you don't have to complete the plan overnight. Feel free to mark each item by whether it's going to be part of phase 1, phase 2, phase 3, etc.

The Baseline:

To quote a certain big-guy chef/bodyguard/deep-voiced goof from the *Emperor's New Groove*, "It's all coming together!" The baseline is the last document in your marketing plan. To understand what the baseline is, I'm going to quickly teach you one of the most valuable tools in my toolbelt for any kind of goal achieving.

I had a mentor once who told me: "If you asked me which tool I would get rid of last if I had to, it would be Baseline Strategy." I didn't really understand the power of the tool at the time and I thought it was kind of a weird thing to say, but I definitely get it now. And I agree with that statement, 100%.

The Baseline Strategy is one of the most powerful concepts I've learned and it can be applied across finances, health, business, relationships, etc. It's based on the premise that whatever result you're receiving in life, is directly proportional to the amount of effort you're putting out in that area. There are a few scenarios we could argue that this doesn't fully apply to, but for the most part, I can't imagine too many people want to argue with me about that premise. Basically, if we were making this an equation, it would look like this:

"Effort = Results"

Now! Let's say that I don't love the results that I'm getting currently and I want to increase my results. No problem. If you remember back to high school algebra when your teacher asked you to solve for X, we learned quickly that whatever we do to one side of the equation, we have to do to the other. So, if we want to increase the results, we have to do the same thing with the effort. The only challenge is that sometimes, we're maxed out on the effort we're putting out. Can I get an Amen? So sometimes we first have to identify what we can remove from the Effort side of the equation. This is the equivalent of reducing your fractions to the lowest common denominator. Once things are less complicated, we can now start adding the things we need to. **This is the stra**tegy **side of t**he **Base**line **Stra**tegy and it can be used to level up how you manage your people, finances, sales, marketing, health, and more.

If the strategy part is the part where we analyze and remove or add effort, the baseline is the actual list of the things you're doing on a recurring basis to produce the result you're producing. This is important because you can't adjust the amount of effort you're putting out if you don't know exactly what that effort includes. *That* is the baseline. It is a list of all the things you're doing on a recurring basis to achieve the result you're achieving. Daily, weekly, monthly, quarterly, annually, etc, if it's being done on a regular basis, it going to go on the baseline.

For example, let's say I wanted to get healthier! This is a pretty common goal, and one I've had on my radar off and on through most of my life. The first place I need to start is by identifying what am I doing to produce the result I'm producing. The answer, most of the time, is "not much." I'm going with the flow. I'm eating whatever is easiest to grab and skipping workouts when I'm too tired. If I want to get my health under control, I might add the following items to my baseline:

1. Plan food intake **daily**
2. Do 10 push-ups **daily**
3. Do 25 squats **daily**
4. Go for a walk **weekly**
5. Go to the gym 2x **weekly**
6. Plan shopping list **weekly**
7. Read a health-focused book **monthly**

We can talk about the feasibility of adding all these things to my baseline simultaneously later (hint: it doesn't work well to change this much at once for the ADHD brain). For now, you can at least see a layout of what needs to be done on a recurring basis. Notice how each of those has a **Daily**, **Weekly**, or **Monthly** assigned frequency? Your baseline should too.

So let's apply this in marketing! The marketing baseline is a list of all the marketing activities you or your team will do on a regular basis, broken out by frequency. This is the list of activities you can evaluate in your monthly CMO meeting (more on that later) to determine if you need to add or subtract from the baseline to stay on track to hit your goals. A sample marketing baseline might look like:

1. Post to social media (YouTube, Instagram, Facebook, LinkedIn) **daily**
2. Review PR requests & respond as applicable **daily**
3. Write blog for website **weekly**
4. Create PR pitch & distribute to PR contacts **weekly**
5. Record long-form videos **monthly**

You can get as detailed or as brief as you want *as long as you're specific*, but now is the time to list out all the things you'll be doing regularly that will help carry the marketing you're building and create the results you're looking for in your small business. Start by looking at all of the tactics you've identified that you want to run and have planned to kick-off in your project plan. Then ask yourself what will you need to do, and how frequently, to keep this tactic rolling? That is the line that goes on your baseline.

Go create a document in your marketing plan folder, call it "Marketing Baseline [Year]" and build it out now.

Ready for the coolest bonus yet? I've got a sample marketing plan uploaded for you at MarketingBeyondSocialMedia.com to compare to your own and use as inspiration on your journey! My recommendation? Go download it now.

A couple of warnings…

Before we wrap up the 3Ms entirely, I do want to lay out a couple of warnings regarding the baseline to help you avoid some of the traps that might pop up!

First, as I mentioned above, be *very* careful about overloading yourself right off the bat. That's usually a bad idea in any capacity, but it's really bad here. Because of the potential of the Baseline Strategy, the last thing you want your brain to start associating it with is failure. If that happens, you will instinctively start avoiding it. It's like going to the gym and trying to lift a 120lbs barbell to do some curls when you haven't stepped foot in the gym in ten years. It's going to tear some things and possibly cause lasting damage!

One of my favorite sayings is, "**Mom**entum **bui**lds!" *So start small*. You can add more down the road. If you aren't doing much of anything on a recurring basis right now, you might start with just two or three things. Notice how I've only got two things listed as "Daily" in my baseline? While this is a sample baseline, that's also pretty close to my actual baseline layout. I'm extremely cautious about setting myself up to have to do anything daily. Mostly because I know I'll get bored pretty quickly and just *not* do it. I actually have my social media broken out two ways on my baseline:

- Create social media posts **weekly**
- Film longform and short videos **monthly**

While I do create short videos for social media throughout the week as I get inspired, I found that if I try to do it daily, it becomes too much and doesn't get done. Same thing with the content. I'd rather let myself sit down once a week and create a bunch of content, then send it off to my graphic designer to create the graphics to go along with it. Then, once a month, I can dedicate four hours to brainstorm a bunch of videos and film them for the entire month. This helps me ensure content is going out regularly, and I'm staying engaged and interested in what I'm doing.

Secondly, if you need to stagger your project plan kick-off by tactic so you can complete the kickoff for one tactic, then start running the one or two baseline items that are associated while you kick off the next tactic over a couple of months, that's okay!

You'll want to make sure you're checking in weekly with your baseline to see how you're doing. I have an "end of week" review recurring on my calendar every Friday where I sit down and I compare actual activities from the week to the goals from my baseline. During this quick weekly recap, I fill out my KPI trackers, and I wrap with some journaling to let go of the week so I can enjoy the weekend. While I'm comparing actual activities to the goals from my baseline, I am looking for any areas where I didn't hit the baseline goals from the previous period as well. If I realize that I'm consistently missing a baseline item, it's time for me to take a good look at that item. Why am I avoiding it? Is it just not producing? Am I trying to do much? Do I need to reduce the frequency? Do I need to adjust the strategy to be more exciting? If it *needs* to be done regardless, (for example I used to have my short video creation as a daily task), do I need to restructure things or tie it to a reward to ensure it does get knocked out consistently?

At least once a month, during the CMO meeting (Yes, I'm still going to talk about this more in a minute!), I will evaluate everything on the baseline to determine what to remove, outsource or add. But I can't do that if I'm not actually executing on the baseline from week-to-week properly!

Deploying Your Marketing Plan

Guess what? If you've been following the powder poofs, you've now got your marketing plan in hand. Congratulations!

In all likelihood, you'll continue evolving the Target Market(s) and the Message at least once a year. The Project Plan and the Baseline now become your day-to-day marketing guidelines. At this point, I will typically go into my project management software and input all the pieces of the project plan into the software, set due dates, and assign out pieces to my team members as appropriate. This is also usually when I go to my calendar to block out at least an hour a week to work on moving those individual projects forward. As a note, to make things easy on myself, I usually copy and paste the notes from the Project Plan into the calendar event so that when I go to look at it, my notes are right there and easy to reference. As a last step, before I'm officially finished with the plan, I will print off my baseline and pin that up where I can see it.

If I'm working with marketing vendors, now is a smart time to send them all a copy of my marketing message and target market(s). I usually also ask those vendors to review these documents and:

1. Make sure everything they are doing for me is taking those into consideration.

2. Let me know if they have any ideas on what else we can do to share this marketing message with this target market.

This is usually when I will also provide instructions for any adjustments I've already noted need to be implemented by that vendor or notify them of any projects I'll need their help with. If I need content first (like for my website developer or my graphic designer), I will let them know when to expect that content and my expected timeline for turnaround of the completed product.

Then I message the appropriate team members to advise them to check the project management software and to let me know if they have any questions. That may seem a little unnecessary since I know the project management software emails them as well, but I want to make sure they know the dialogue is open for questions. Not only that, but I prefer to send that reminder inside the platform that they are most likely to use to ask those questions. It just makes it psychologically easier for them to reach out in the same channel if they do come up with questions once they look at the assignment. They may *know* in their heads that they can reach out with questions, but I've found if I don't do a quick reminder, sometimes they just don't. That usually leads to projects not being completed on time or to the quality I expected. It's just easier to be proactive and send a quick message.

DEPLOY YOUR MARKETING PLAN NOW:

1. Add tasks to your project management software if applicable
2. Block time on your calendar to work on your projects
3. Contact your vendors
4. Alert staff of assignments

An Important Note:

In this next section I'm going to discuss some strategies, lessons learned, and tools that (in my opinion) are dangerous to worry about implementing too early in the process. This section is designed to help you identify opportunities for incremental improvement and level up your marketing. These are *not* tactics I recommend for anyone who is just getting going. Not to be mean or 'gatekeep' anything but simply because of two things I mentioned earlier:

1. Small Changes Are Sustainable

2. Momentum Builds

When we start getting too deep too fast, it becomes overwhelming. That overwhelm leads to failure to take action. Without action, nothing happens. That overwhelm also leads to small business owners panicking over the need to run A/B tests instead of just getting stuff out there. You can't A/B test something that has absolutely *no traction*. I personally feel like the concepts I'm going to share next are how you'll take the marketing plan you have created to the next level. But for that to be true, you have to be at some level of marketing sufficiency. These are not critical to getting your marketing off the ground.

If you identify with any of the following categories, I would recommend putting a pin in this chapter and skipping ahead to the **Wrap-up chapter on Page 141.**
You can come back to the next chapter when you match the second set of guidelines.

1.

Skip this next chapter (for now) if you are:

• Just getting your first marketing plan completed and looking to get it rolling

• You are responsible for doing all of your marketing and not ready or able to outsource any pieces yet

2.

Read this next chapter if you fit any of the following categories:

• Have been marketing for a while, are getting good results, are looking for an extra edge, and are not overwhelmed by everything you've read so far.

• Your marketing message is well deployed, generating engagement from your audience and you're putting out consistent messages.

• OR you're functioning as the strategist of your marketing and have a team to help with the nitty gritty details of execution.

Level Up

If I were a video gamer, I'm sure I'd have some kind of funny pun to put here. But I'm not, so let's just get going! There is one incredibly important lesson that I want to dig into here that is a game changer in terms of the exponential marketing concept we explored earlier: The Brand Ecosystem. I referenced the Brand Ecosystem earlier but I didn't dig in nearly as far as I'm about to. It took me a long, long time to learn this one. In practicality, if your marketing isn't already getting some traction, this is a lot of work that isn't going to generate much new business. If your marketing *is* getting traction, this is how you are going to convert a higher number of the people coming in contact with your brand.

We're going to dig into three pieces here:

1. The Brand Ecosystem
2. Recapturing the Escapees
3. Analytics

The Brand Ecosystem

The best way to think of the Brand Ecosystem is like a black hole. Growing up as a kid, I had three major fears:

1. Quicksand would swallow me alive
2. Rodents Of Unusual Size were a real thing (thanks Princess Bride!)
3. A black hole would swallow me!

Ok, there was probably a fourth that I'd say or do something mortifyingly embarrassing. But that one was more likely to come true and therefore somehow less terrifying than the first three. I realize now that none of these were real problems, but somewhere along the way, I got the idea that Quicksand and Black

Holes were going to be a much bigger problem than they are today. Those and the Bermuda Triangle. Seriously! As a kid, I wondered many times why no one had tried to solve that problem. Cue the eyeroll at my younger self.

I have no clue where the idea that black holes were out there, waiting to just suck you into them sparked. But it was there. Probably Star Trek if I'm honest. Either way, we all know what a black hole is, at least in theory. It's this giant section of nothingness that sucks everything in around it and it's impossible to escape. Many a Doctor Who and Star Trek episodes revolve around that universally recognized trope, and there probably *should* be more of them around than there are.

While your brand eco-system isn't really a 'black hole' in the terrifying sense, this is a great analogy that makes a lot of sense. You want your brand to be so appealing, so inviting, and so seamless in how it transitions viewers from one page to another on the website, or from content to content on your social media, that no one wants to leave. Simply put: when a prospect finds your business, they should be drawn deeper and deeper, feeling engaged, inspired, motivated, learning, intrigued, etc.

We already know that the more time someone spends with your brand, the more likely they are to buy from you. This is why consultants and coaches offer webinars and speaking. They know that once they've been able to talk to someone for 60+ minutes, the likelihood that person will buy from the consultant is high. So our job, as the marketers of our business, is to make sure that once someone is exposed to our brand, *they get hooked*. At no point in time should they realize how much time they've been spending on your website or scrolling your social media. That means that nothing can be boring or bland and everything should lead to something else.

Imagine getting someone to visit your website from the article you were quoted in. If the website is well designed, it should draw them from page to page with ease. It might encourage them to go check out your YouTube channel, or LinkedIn, but those should draw them back to the website. Each page on the website should lead to the logical next page, and the next, and the next. All while trying to get them closer and closer to that brand engagement indicator we talked about in the Customer Journey.

To be clear: not everything has to include a call to action to buy something. Sometimes that call to action is a subtly placed hint to check out another article with a, "If you liked this article, you'll love [...]." As long as the next article is relevant to the previous one, and interesting to the reader, you can draw them to the next one, and the next. The longer you can keep them circulating in your cloud of "brand-ness," the more likely they are to opt-in and the more likely they are to buy.

So go look at your website. Look through every single page and, if you have time, every single blog post.

When you get to the bottom, does it lead them somewhere else? If not, this is what we call a dead-end. It's not a good thing. Every page on your website should lead them somewhere else. How about your social media? Is it enticing them to dig deeper? Even if it's just "Sparked by the post we made last week…" Does it draw them back towards your website every so often?

And there's another side to the Brand Ecosystem that we haven't touched on yet: everything should support everything else. Does your social media talk about the other marketing that you're doing to give a sense that you have a broader reach? I.e. are you showcasing pictures from that event you participated in last week? Showing off the features from all the PR placements feature you?

As I shared before, one of the most successful marketing campaigns I ever ran with my corporate job happened because the client used us as social proof. He splashed, "As Seen on [our website name]" on everything else they put out. If he had an ad running, it was featured in the corner. It was on their social media cover photos. It was on the website. On their Google listing. He made sure that every single marketing tactic was referenced and showcased on all others, and vice versa. He used his page on our website to feature his social media and other PR placements too. If your marketing isn't referencing, "As Seen on/with _____" you're leaving some instant credibility on the table.

Word of warning: There's a level of "Cool" and there's a level of "Wow… they're reaching!" that you want to be on guard against. What do I mean? Well, have you ever seen someone's website that says, "As seen on" but you don't recognize any of the logos and half of them have a distinctly "eh" vibe about them? You know the ones I'm talking about. The colors are a little unusual, not in a good way, and it's too busy. That poor logo has more elements crammed into it than a New York subway at rush hour. Those logos don't bring the same level of trust as an "As Seen on CNBC" graphic. That is not the way to do this.

But a banner that says, "TikTok's Favorite Baseball Team," (I couldn't resist one last Savannah Bananas reference) or has, "As Seen/Heard On" sections that has at least a few recognizable logos goes a long way. Don't be afraid to insert "Check us out on _____" and insert another platform onto the home page of your website. Just make sure that outbound link takes them to a place that also links them back to the website eventually. Even "Member of" badges can go a long way to build trust and make you look more impressive and far reaching than you might actually be. Let your marketing work together. Yes, you might have to update the website if you leave that group or lose the certification or placement. But you're going to be more proactive about your website anyhow at this point. Edits happen. They are actually good for your search engine rankings. This is one of the reasons that I recommend businesses that are early in their lifespan use template programs. Once you're a little larger, it's not cost prohibitive to get a web master to go in and make minor edits. If you're not there, programs like Wix or Strikingly are extremely easy to make edits on, even for the most un-tech-savvy among us.

The long and short of this is that marketing doesn't function well in a vacuum. Your outbound campaigns and online placements should leverage that you're listed elsewhere. Your prospecting funnels should leverage existing content like emails, posts, videos, etc in the early outreach and inspire them to check out the actual posts and enter the brand ecosystem. Your memberships should be shouted from the sky.

Most importantly here, everything should lead to something else.

Recapturing the Escapees....

That header makes this sound a little villainous. It's not wholly intended that way, but my inner wanted-to-be-the-villain-in-every-play child is maybe a little too pleased about the thought. Ultimately, you're not going to keep everyone inside your ecosystem all the time. People are going to leave. Sometimes before they get to the initial contact, even if they *were* a good candidate. It's not always your fault. But there are things you can do to get them to come back.

There are two groups you'll want to ensure you're drawing back into your fold regularly:

Good fit prospects who either just didn't decide yet or aren't ready to buy yet

Buyers who already bought and are ready for the next level, or to buy again

The second group is markedly easier to pull back in. If they already bought, you should have an email or some form of contact to stay in touch. You can invite them to engage with your social media and check out new content on your website that way. It's the first group that requires a little more thought. This is the group that things like retargeting ads were built for.

If you don't have an emailing list started already, now's the time. Go back through the lists of everyone who has bought from you and get their name and email address into a spreadsheet. Depending on how long it's been since they bought from you, you might want to send an initial, "Hey! I'm starting an emailing list and here's why you want to stay on the list!" email. But if it hasn't, get them on the list. They gave you their contact info. They bought from you once. They probably want to hear from you again.

Next, retargeting. I mentioned before that these can be especially helpful for whatever you identify as the Brand Engagement Indicator page on your website. There are ways to set up retargeting ads yourself but it can be complex. If you aren't up for it, find someone you trust who can do it for you. Unless you have a massive amount of website traffic, you can probably keep your retargeting budget under $100/month. It's not a lot of money, but it's a game-changing level strategy to keep you on their mind.

One of the big keys for retargeting to work is a recognizable brand and a simple message. You've got one fraction of a corner of their brain that will notice you. That's great! Your only goal in that ad is to get them back to your website. Unless you're selling products online that are a quick and easy decision, *this ad is not going to sell anything for you*. This ad should be designed to draw them back to your website. The design and colors should get their attention. The message should entice them to click. Remember from the very beginning about the psychology of conversions? Focus on one thing at a time.

"How will I get their attention?" (colors and design)

THEN

"How will I get them back to the website?" (text and call to action)

For example, I've done retargeting ads that promote our events. They perform at a mediocre level. The ads where I promote a specific article that would appeal to the ideal buyer, or a freebie if they come back to the site perform much, much better.

Data and Analytics

This is the last of the Level Up tools I want to talk about and this is definitely in the category of leveling up what you're currently doing. Data and analytics will allow you to take what's currently happening and understand what's working and what isn't. Armed with this information, you can put more emphasis on what's working and cut the things that aren't. But there's a dark side to these analytics that I'll talk about in just a minute (hence why it's in this chapter). In other words, as you're reading the next section, if you're finding yourself getting overwhelmed, skip to the next chapter and come back later.

Before we get to that though, there are a few important references I'll be using here that I want to define just in case they are new to you!

Google Analytics – When I reference Google Analytics with both terms and capitalized, I'm referring to a free service from Google that can be installed on your website. This powerful tool collects info on how people are finding you, where they are going on your site, how long they stay, how many visitors you have, etc. I tend to favor Google Analytics data over a platform's built-in dashboards (like Wix, Strikingly, Shopify, Square, etc) just because I've found that Google Analytics tends to be the most accurate and consistent.

Search Console - Also a free service from Google. Once this is installed on your website, it will collect info about what search phrases you're ranking for and getting clicks under. It will also tell you how many impressions you have in the overall search engine results and your click-thru-rate. It's a pretty fantastic tool!

Heatmap - This is a piece of software that can be installed on your website that will track where people are looking by tracking the mouse (which most of us use to guide our eyes on the page) when they visit your site. There are lots of software that can do this. As mentioned before, it's not really an invasion of privacy because it's not tied to any one specific visitor. So I have no idea where any one person went. But using this software, I can see the trends. These software change over time so I'll keep my current favorite option listed at MarketingBeyondSocialMedia.com.

Remember when I mentioned that there's a dark element to the data and analytics side of marketing? This is the side of marketing that has the most potential to be intimidating and to become a black hole for you *in a bad way*. It's easy, once you start getting into the analytics, to spiral into trying to figure out every single visitor to your website or impressions on a post that didn't get engagement. So let's start by establishing one important thing: *you're never going to win them all*. You won't win every visitor to your site. If you can get to a 10-20% conversion rate on your site, that's pretty decent! If you are getting a solid reach in comparison to your total followers and engagement from even a tenth of your followers on social media, that's pretty good. If you get a 1-3% click-thru-rate on your retargeting ads, that's great.

Don't obsess over winning the war on data and analytics. Instead, use them to focus your marketing. Look at your Google Analytics to determine which pages are getting the most traffic. Then analyze those pages to determine how you can tweak them to increase conversions. Use Search Console to inspire your content and adjust your current website to rank higher. My rule of thumb is that I am only allowed to spend seven minutes reviewing analytics per website to look for what information is in there. At that point I pick three numbers I want to improve and make a plan that I think will help. But at the end of the month, I'm not allowed to obsess over what happened. If it worked, great. If it didn't, I'll try something else.

For example: The Grow Disrupt website has always ranked very highly for the search term Business Operator on Google. This is vestigial from back when we had a series of three pages focusing on the different levels of business owners (Job Owner, Business Operator, Business Owner). The goal with these pages was to help visitors identify which level they wanted to be at, and subsequently which event was meant for them. Eventually, we realized that we wanted to do events pretty much exclusively for Business Operators, retired the events that were built for the other two categories and hid the pages on the website.

Hid them, but did not delete them in case we ever wanted to bring them back. Notably, we left them visible to the search engines. Then one month I started to notice that we were getting a lot of clicks to the Business Operator page on the website through Google Analytics. When I went into Search Console, I realized that we'd ranked up for the search term "Business Operator." But that while that page was highly visited, no one was transitioning to any other pages on the website. That told me that the content and design weren't working for us and prompted an overhaul of the entire page. At time of writing, we just rolled out an updated version of the page and we'll continue to track the analytics closely to see if the page is doing a better job transitioning visitors to other places on the website. If you'd like to check it out, you can at GrowDisrupt.com/business-operator. If trying to type that link into your browser is giving you trouble, I've also linked to it from MarketingBeyondSocialMedia.com

A secondary example. Google Analytics offers something called the Engagement Score (which used to be called the Bounce Rate). This is an overview of how long someone hung out on your website and looked around. In an ideal world, this would be a solid 5-10 minute number. In reality, most websites are trying to get up over a minute. So when I'm working on a website and see that the engagement score is 15 seconds, I might first look to see what the most popular pages are. Then I can evaluate them to find three ways that I think I can increase engagement and therefore improve the Engagement Score. For example, I might check my heatmap software to see at what point on the page do I lose the most visitors and add buttons or try to redesign that section of the page to create curiosity to keep scrolling. The next month, I'll check in again, and try again. It's not likely I'll take it to 60-seconds+ in a single month, but if I see that it's improved to 18 or 20 seconds, I know not to change what I did, but maybe to add something else.

One thing to keep in mind is that there are a lot of variables coming into play in analytics. There are a hundred reasons the Engagement Score didn't improve. It may have nothing to do with my efforts. There are a hundred reasons someone didn't click my retargeting ad. I can't obsess over it. It *will* end poorly.

Use heatmaps that show you where people are clicking or checking out on the website to adjust your site design. Use Google Analytics and Search Console to find out how people are finding you and leverage it more. Use Google Analytics and heatmaps to find out what pages on the website are losing the most people and then adjust them to keep those people in your brand ecosystem. Cater to the search terms that you want to rank for by creating articles, blogs and website content that revolve around those terms. Then watch Search Console to see if it works. If it does, great. If it doesn't, try something else next month.

Ultimately, if you aren't already driving traffic and engagement, there aren't enough analytics to be worth the time to understand. Focus on that first rather than getting caught up in analytics and trying to get 'perfect' content out (remember, no silver bullets!). Also, it doesn't help to panic because you don't understand every single number in the Google Analytics dashboard. Pick one to learn, start googling it, ask questions in forums and groups, and then continue tweaking until you get it where you want to go. Then do that again with another number and another. I know that we, especially my fellow ADHD entrepreneurs, want stuff done *now*. We'd rather hire someone to do all this for us and do it perfectly the first time. But it's not going to make as big a difference as you think it will. Marketing is a long game that you have to be committed to learning and improving over time.

Take a deep breath, take it slow, you got this.

Closing

To bring this full circle to "Lessons I've learned on the violin that also apply to marketing": playing notes for the sake of playing notes is useless. Even when I'm practicing scales, my goal is not *just* to hit the note but to improve my playing. To notice how the sound changes as I change directions on the string or change strings with the bow. If I really want to make an impact when I'm playing on the violin, I need to bring passion in so the music can truly sing. There's an example I use nearly every time I talk about marketing and I'm going to do my best to recreate it here in the pages of this book.

When I first take the stage to talk marketing, after preliminaries are finished, I will almost always pick up the violin and play the same song, two ways for the audience. Once, exactly as it's written. Hitting the notes exactly as they are listed and holding them for the exact amount of time intended. I follow the dynamics that the composer listed exactly. It is beautiful, but empty. The next time I play, I will pour my heart into the piece. I look for the phrasing so the piece can breathe and come alive. I'm playing the same piece, with the same notes, pacing, dynamics, etc, but this time, it always feels different. I bring in the artist's choice of vibrato to make the piece feel faster or slower. Richer here. Frantic there. Most importantly, I allow myself to experience the emotion of the piece. In doing so, it sparks emotion in the audience as well.

When I ask the audience which version they liked better the answer is always the same: the second.

We know that emotion makes a world of difference. I already discussed this from the perspective of adding value, but I want to dig a little deeper. We know that emotion is memorable. We know that passion matters. And yet we get so caught up in trying to push out marketing that we forget to tap into the very heart of humanity: emotion. As we discussed previously, small business owners often focus on educating, assuming someone will feel enlightened when they read it. But that's not guaranteed because many times, they didn't even read it! We have to spark emotion first and draw them in. Then we have the platform to educate.

Just like playing notes for the sake of playing them is a waste of time, pushing out marketing for the sake of marketing won't work either. This is why I have repeatedly stressed that we have to do things we love, that energize us. We can do more because of the energy advantage, *and* we get better results. Focus on how you can bring passion to your play. Because **passion pulls your prospect to you. It sparks something incredible. It makes you memorable. It feels authentic. It builds trust. It makes an impact.**

Over the years, I've found that the violin teaches me business better than pretty much anyone else, as long as I *listen*. One thing it's consistently taught me is that I cannot apply equal pressure or weight to all the strings. If I use the same amount of weight in the bow on the E string (the tiny one on the right side of the violin) as I do on the G string (the big fat one on the left side), it will sound horrendous. Taking it further, if I shift up into a higher position on the violin where my hand is closer to the bridge in order to play higher notes on the same string, and do not adjust my weight and speed with the bow to compensate, it sounds terrible. There's a lot of power in recognizing that every time I change strings or positions, I need to adjust to accommodate.

The same is true with my marketing. I have to adjust how I'm delivering my marketing message based on the platform I'm using. There has to be some consistency. I'm still going to hit the actual notes and use the bow to make music for the most part, just like I'm going to use the same brand and overall messaging. But I'm going to adjust to accommodate the changing elements. In other words, my messaging is going to be the same. But how I show it may be different. I may be able to get away with using a bunch of different colors for the text on my website to say, "I understand you! Your brain needs colors!" But putting that many different font colors on a graphic to post on social media may look remedial and childish. I may be able to use a funny, sketch-style video inside of YouTube shorts, but find that it falls short on LinkedIn. TV ads don't translate well to radio. And vice versa! I understand the temptation to try and disperse your message across as many platforms as possible. We live in a world where people are constantly telling you to leverage content creation fifteen different ways.

Here's the challenge I have with that: If I'd tried to learn all the nuances of playing the violin at once, I would have been reduced to a puddle. If you're trying to be everywhere, everything, all at once, so will you. It's far better to really focus and get really good at one or two things, then add another. This way you can learn to understand the nuance of playing on that string or that platform. Then you can add another. And another. And another as we discussed before. This is not to say you *can't* have your podcast cut up into shorts to use as well and get good results. You just can't do it if you don't even have a podcast because you're paralyzed with overwhelm by how to do it all at once. You're also not necessarily going to get good results until you've had time to really learn the best practices for shorts. So relax. You probably don't need to drive tons of traffic right off the bat anyhow while you're still getting comfortable behind the mic. Besides that, the most episodes you release now, the more of those shorts you can grab later to promote past episodes to current listeners to build the stickiness factor as they absorb more and more from you.

So just get one or two platforms or tactics going at a time. Revise. Refine. Redistribute (the workload to someone else to keep running). Repeat.

Which leads me to one of my favorite concepts to close my speeches with: The power of taking ACTION. We've known for a long time that knowledge is not power anymore. Applied knowledge is power. Knowing stuff is pointless. I had a million product ideas as a kid. I never even looked into how to pursue making them a reality. Likewise, I can't count the number of times someone has come to me to swear that they've got the idea that is going to change the world. But they don't do anything with it. Here's the problem: Ideas and knowledge are useless. It's what you do with it that matters.

Because **ACTION** is an acronym that stands for:

Achieve
Considerable
Traction
In
Objective
Nailing

Did you know that when you take action, you create traction that will bring you closer to the objectives you're aiming to hit? When you fail to take action, you accept your current state of existence. And I get it! It's easy to do that. What we have today hasn't killed us (yet). So our brains, that supercomputer in our heads that is 100% focused on keeping us alive, convince us to keep doing what we're doing.

But it's not working for you, is it? Or you wouldn't have picked up this book. You have a bigger goal, a bigger dream. A passion that is driving you. You care about what you're doing and the people it's impacting. I know because I know the kind of person I built my brand to attract. I know there's a high likelihood that you *are* that kind of person.

We have to take action with what we learn. Run. Review. Revise. Repeat. I do this when playing the violin where I will record myself playing a section, then adjust from there. You can do the same with what you've learned here.

Go to your calendar and create a recurring two-hour block for the last business day of each month and title it "Monthly CMO Meeting"

(See! I promised I'd talk more about this later!). Inside of these two hours, you're going to do just three things:

1. **Review What You** Have **Been Doing** - this is your analytics for the website, social media, tracking for numbers or QR codes and/or reports from your marketing vendors.
2. **Research Potential Marketing Ideas** - this is all the ideas that have been thrown at you throughout the month by sales reps or well-intentioned colleagues, vendors, or even members of your own team.
3. **Plan Adjustments** - cancel stuff that isn't working, build a new project plan (including planning to outreach to vendors to request adjustments if needed), and update your baseline to both remove items that aren't working and add items that are. Then set aside time on your calendar to do the work that you know you need to do!

Bonus! This monthly meeting has been my secret weapon for avoiding getting caught up in the hype of chatting with a sales rep or colleague's excitement and committing to a marketing tactic that isn't going to work for me. I get bombarded with suggestions for platforms to engage with, software to implement, and more weekly. I'm sure you do too. I know those people are (mostly) well intentioned and excited to share what they've found. I was always afraid, if I didn't look at it right away, I would forget (fair enough with my ADHD!). So I would look at it in the heat of the moment and, if it looked good overall, I'd sign up. I found myself overleveraged and pulled in too many directions too many times.

Now, when someone has an idea for me, I go to my calendar and add whatever that idea is to the CMO Meeting calendar event in the description under "Ideas to Research." This allows me to evaluate it in comparison to the rest of my baseline and have a clear head when I'm considering it. Recently this saved me from a program that looked great in theory but didn't fit the rest of my marketing. After reviewing, I realized it would have been a wasted $100/month for a year or longer before I finally thought to cancel it. I know that isn't *much* money in the grand scheme of things. But when you're marketing on $0-$500/month and when the monthly CMO Meeting has saved me from those mistakes again and again and again, it adds up.

The CMO meeting is also probably one of my best tools for staving off the guilt that starts to arise when I see a marketing idea or opportunity. I know I'll evaluate it at the right time and place so I can only implement the stuff I know will make the greatest impact.

The very last thing I want to revisit is one of the first, and most powerful concepts, I brought to the table: Marketing Demands Investment and Craves Creativity.

We already explored the "Demands Investment" part. And throughout this book, we've also explored a lot of the "Craves Creativity" side. But I don't want you to lose sight of the power here. At the end of the day, it's creativity that allows us to create marketing that works on small budgets. Creativity that makes a piece of marketing memorable. Creativity that catches the eye of the passer-by. The smaller your budget, the more creative you have to be. But that same scrappiness will open some amazing doors that will feed other parts of your marketing. Recall the Capri example? Their mascot came about because we were given the challenge of setting up a booth for <$500. And now Teodoro is on the verge of getting his own Instagram account because he is so popular!

There are literally millions of marketing messages being distributed hourly. Your job is to stand out in a sea of chaos. You can't do that if you're doing the same thing as everyone else. If your website looks the same as everyone else.

Your videos.

Your content.

Your messaging.

Your delivery.

I know this is hard. And I frequently get told, "Steph, I wish I was as creative as you!" To bare my soul for a minute, it breaks my heart every time I hear that. I'm not here to make others feel worse about themselves. I believe we are all incredible with unbelievable potential. We all bring such varied experiences and perspectives to the table. It's beautiful. I want to inspire you with what can be. Not intimidate you by where I am today. I've spent so much time cultivating my creativity, I just did it in secret at first because I wasn't good at it.

I think what we forget is that creativity is a muscle and just like the muscles in our bodies, we have to cultivate that muscle. Most important is to remember that creativity rarely happens in isolation. It almost never happens when we're fighting to make something happen. It never happens when we're burnt out from working insane hours.

Creativity comes as a tiny wisp of smoke across the corners of your consciousness. It doesn't shout. You have to learn to listen to it. And to recognize that you're going to be a little clumsy with it right off the bat. That's okay. Keep trying. Keep working. Put that idea out there and see how it goes. Then do another. Then another. Take time to sit and listen to your creative inner voice. And get out of your box. Go for a walk. Go out in nature. Sit down with others regularly to work on your marketing. Get around other people to get ideas from them. Join a Marketing Spark Lab if you're feeling entirely uninspired and want to get some other insights to jumpstart your creativity. The truth is that building a marketing plan is easy. It's finding a way to stand out and the ongoing work to implement, learn, and adjust that is hard.

But there are resources available. There are people who want to see you succeed. Find a group to join that you can lean on. Get around other people who are heading for the stars just like you.

You and your business are worth it.

THESTEPHANIESCHELLER.COM

Printed in the USA
CPSIA information can be obtained
at www.ICGtesting.com
LVHW060810140124
768916LV00041B/1598